I0473405

Out to Lunch

Animal Cartoons

First Printing February 12, 2013
Paperback Edition
ISBN: 978-0-9848872-2-4

Published by
Diesslin Press, Dayton, Ohio
info@the-cartoonist.com

i

Introduction

About "Out To Lunch" Cartoons:

The idiom "Out to Lunch" (OTL) means crazy or out of touch with the reality, so that seemed a fitting strip name for my single-panel general comic. OTL cartoons have been around for more than a decade in various forms and various media including newspapers, magazines, on the internet at the-cartoonist.com and on merchandise. If you haven't heard of them before, that's not surprising since the plethora of media outlets still only reach a limited audience. Hopefully you'll see them more and more in the future and you can find them weekly at the-cartoonist.com. Out to Lunch cartoons are now syndicated and appear in Funnies Extra! papers across the country as well as in more and more newspapers, so hopefully you'll have a chance to see them in their native habitat.

About this Book:

This book takes an exclusive look at OTL animal cartoons, featuring over 155, including some bonus cartoons from some of my other projects (KNOTS Scout cartoons and the Cartoon Old Testament and Cartoon Gospels).

About the Cartoonist:

If a picture is worth a thousand words, a caricature must be worth at least half of that, so here's my self-caricature. If you've seen this, you'll probably agree it's best to leave it at this!

Thank you for your interest in this collection of my *Out to Lunch* (OTL) animal cartoons. I hope you enjoy this second OTL book with over 155 of animal cartoons.

All the best,
Rich

Rich Diesslin
Cartoonist

List of Figures

Bats, Bears, Beavers, Birds and Bugs

Who's Batty

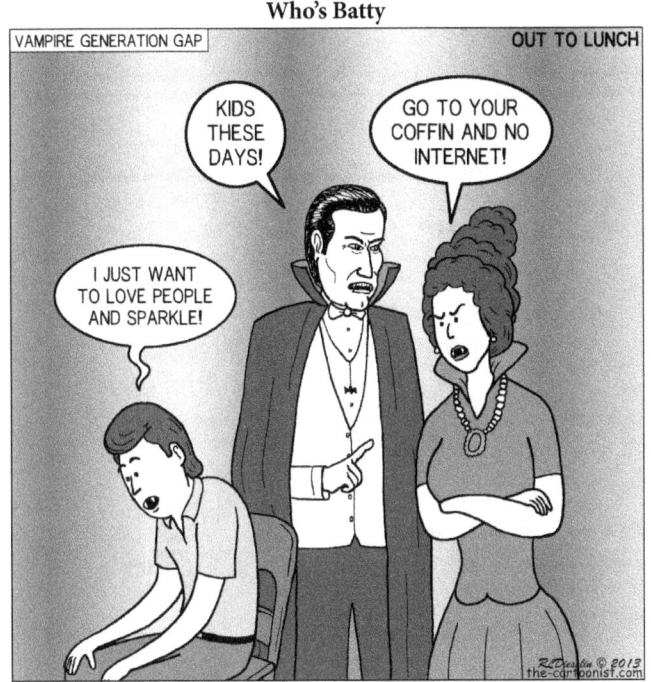

Bat Phone

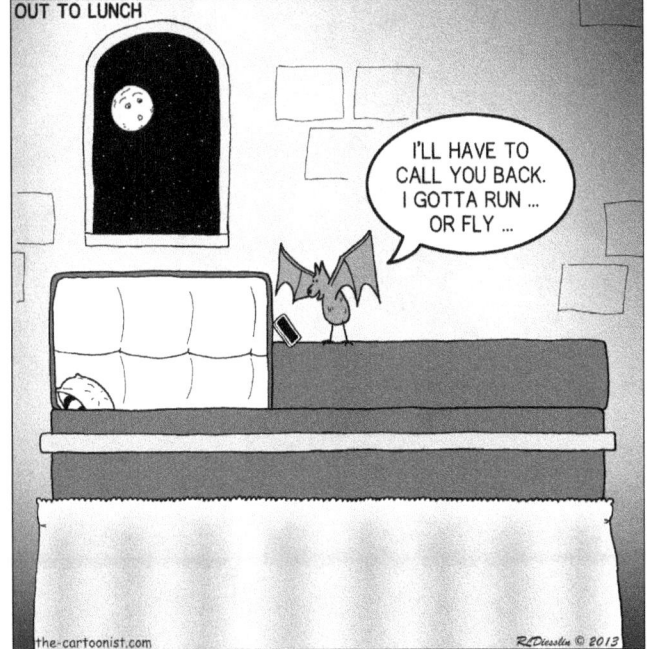

The Dark Knight Rises

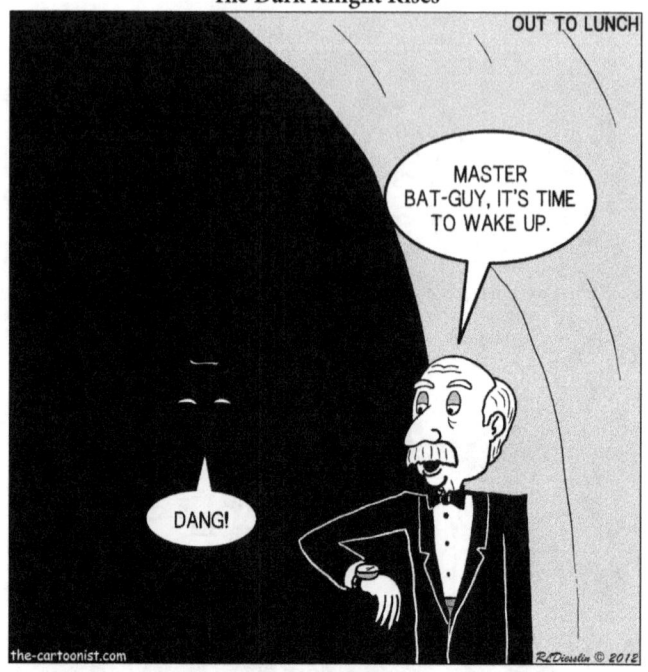

Bear Necessities

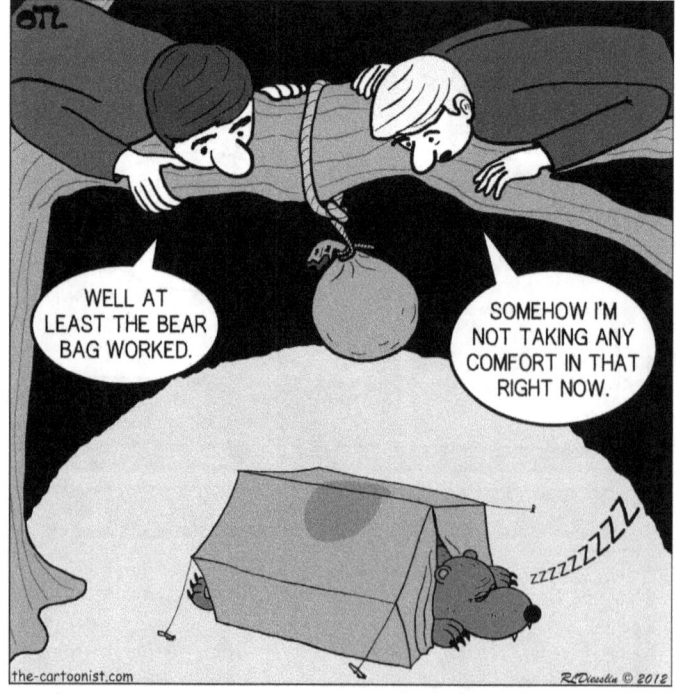

Out to Lunch - Bats, Bears, Beavers, Birds and Bugs - 6

Bearly Kayaking

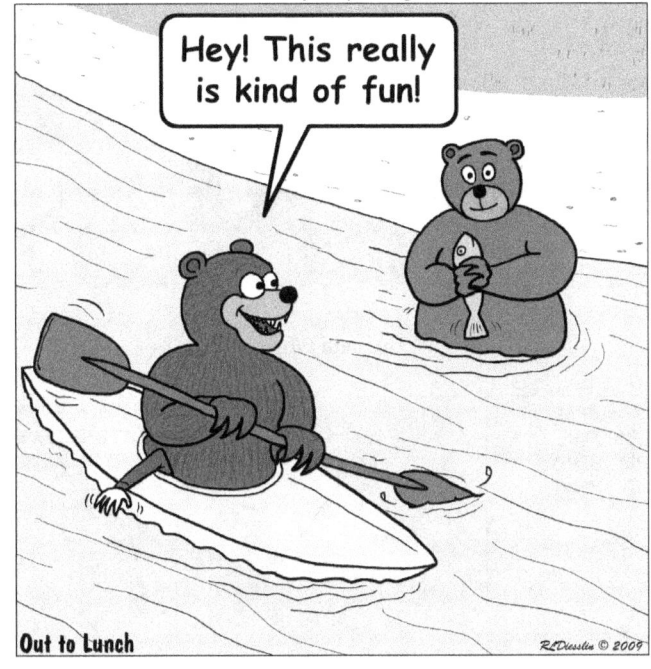

Beaver's Bad Day

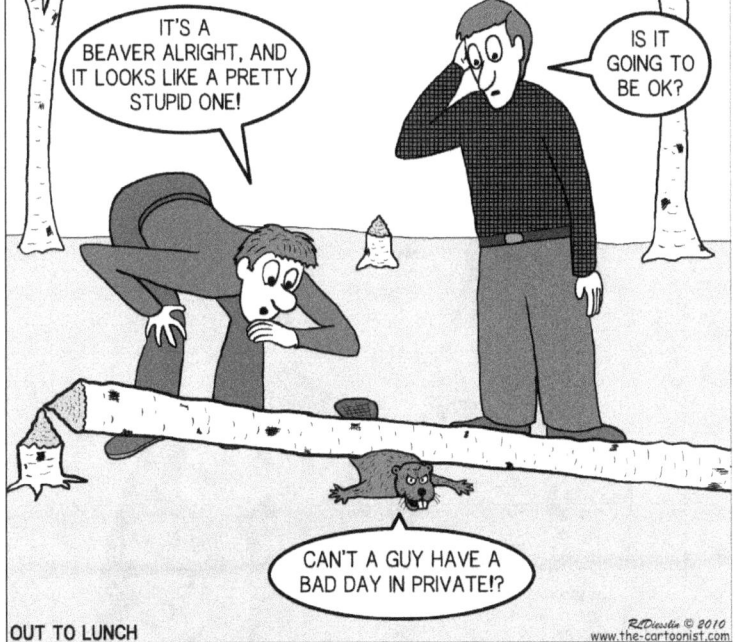

The Late Bird

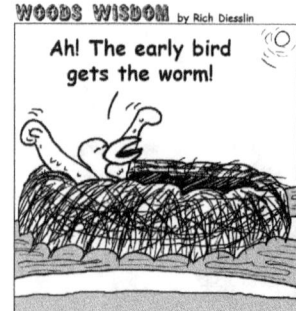
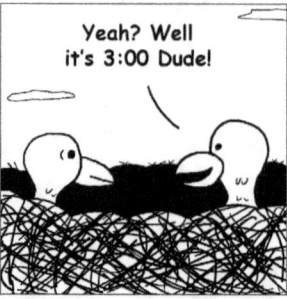
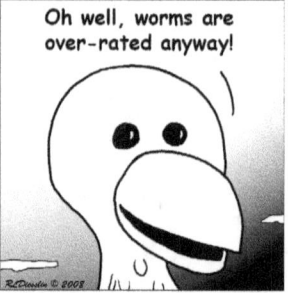

The Late Worm

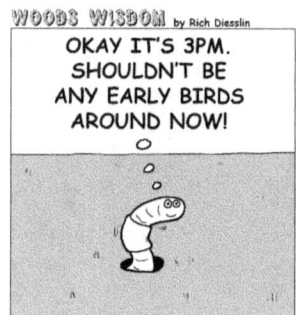
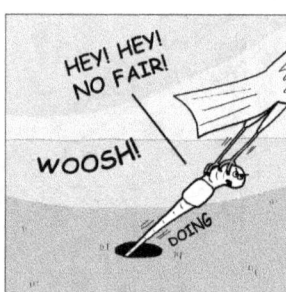
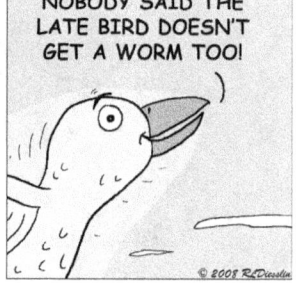

Finger Lickin' Good

Baby It's Cold Outside

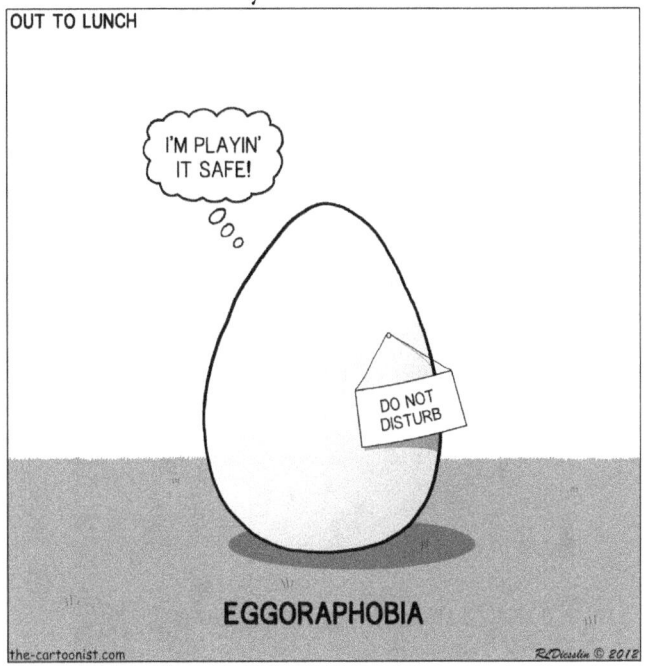

Birds of a Feather

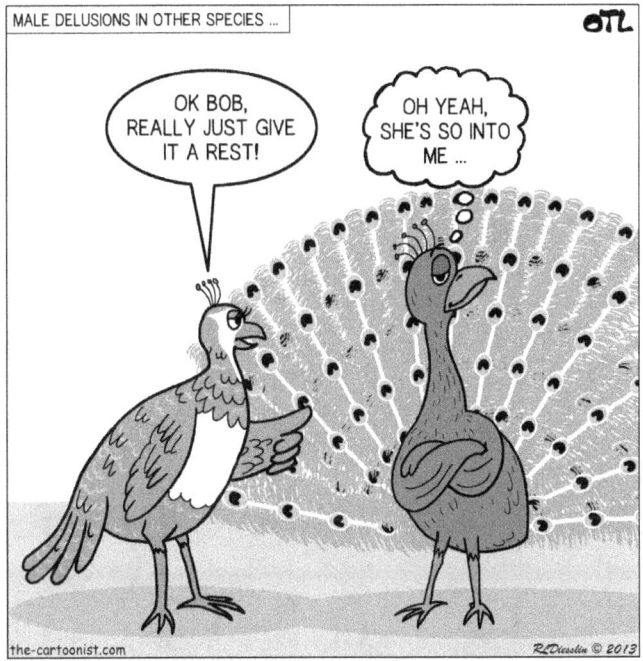

Who's Beeping Now Baby

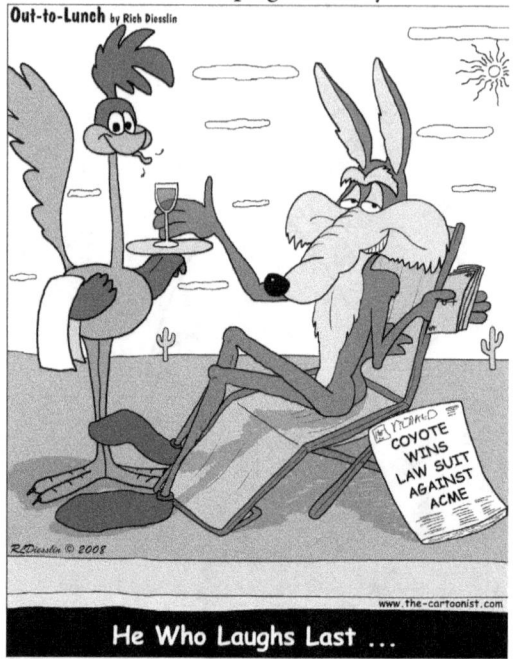

Happy Mother's Day

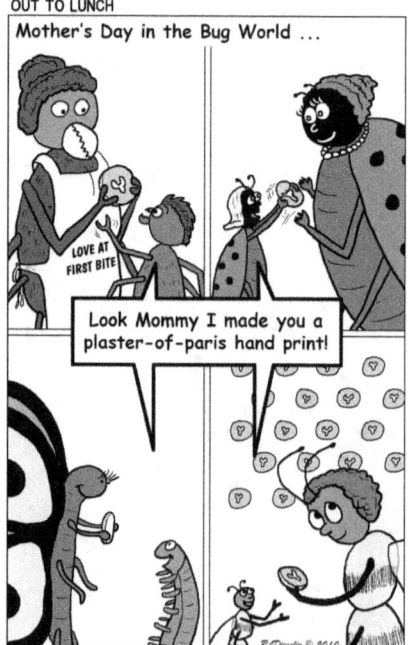

Buzzard Faux Pas

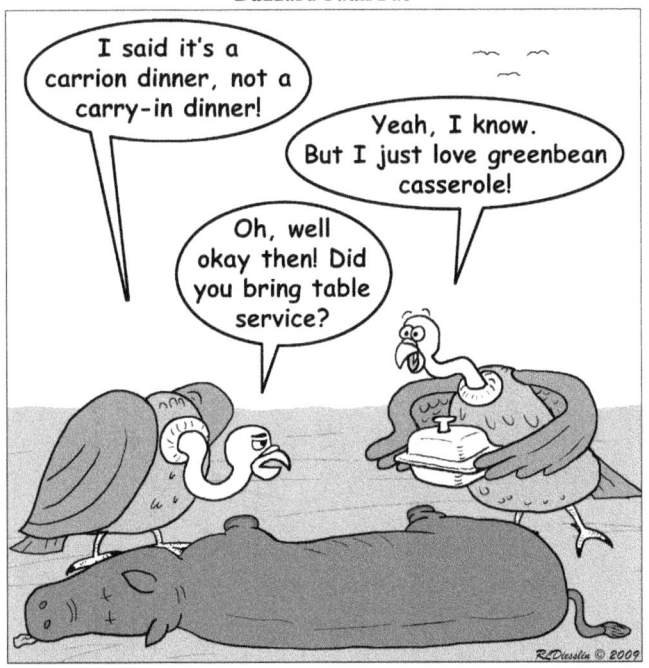

Everybody Likes Pizza

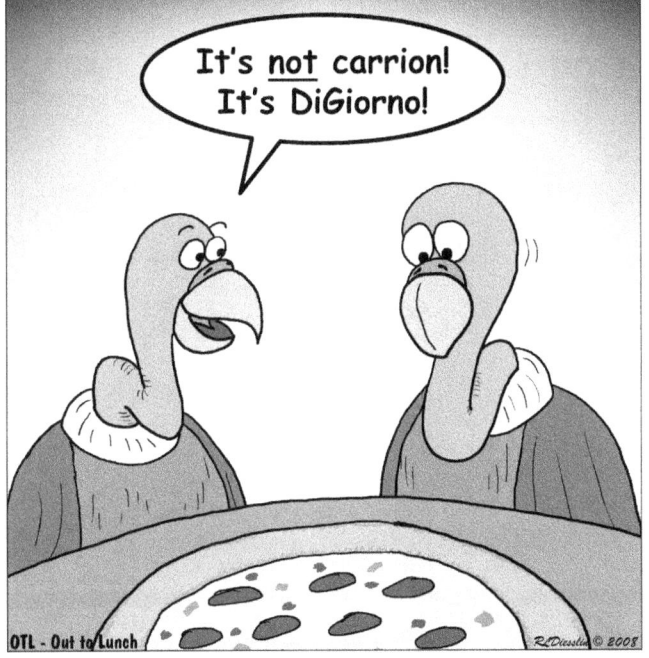

Cats, Cows, Crocs and Gators

Human Car Rides

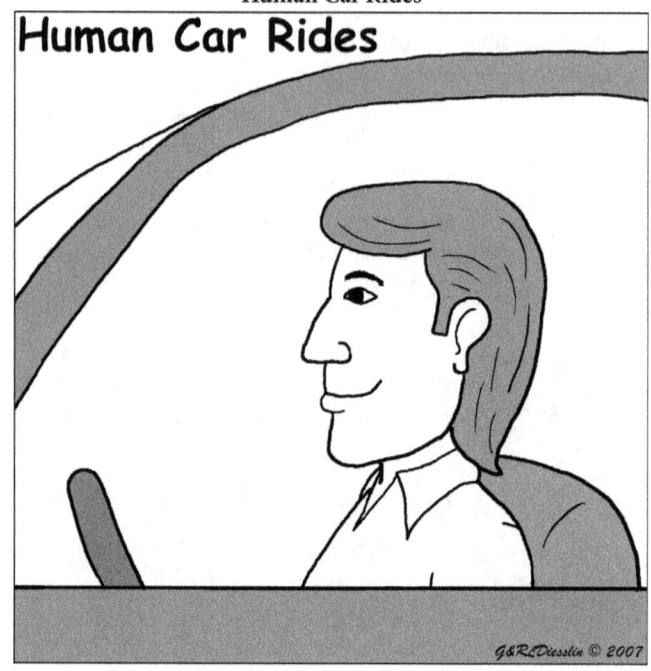

Dog Car Rides

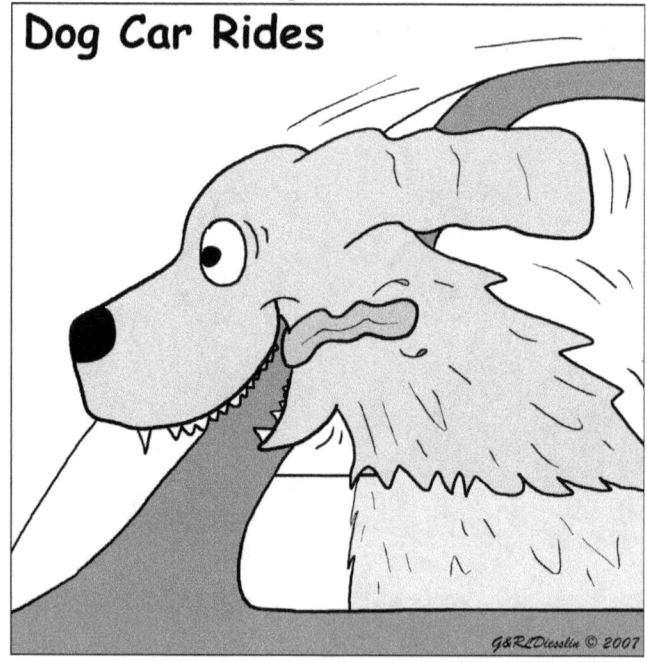

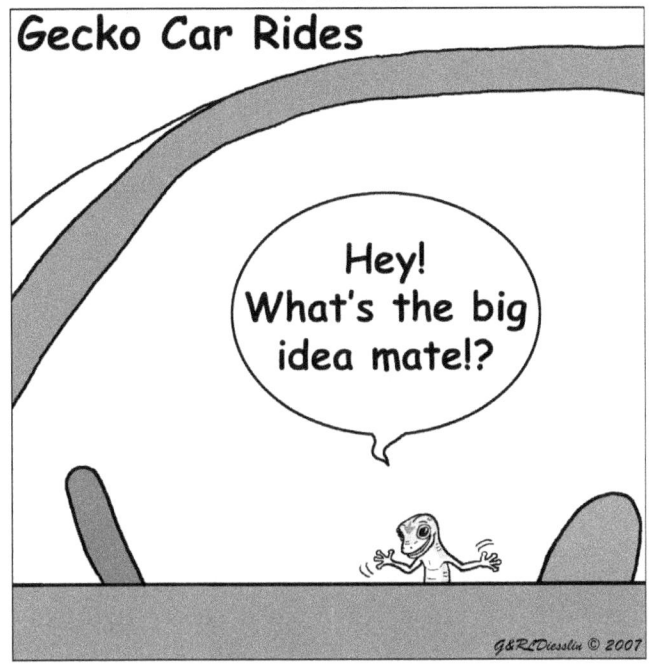

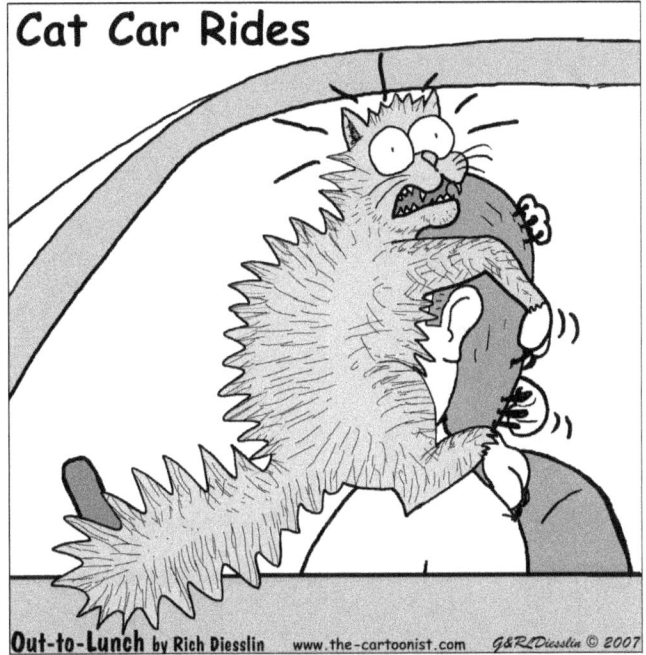

Scottish Cat Calls

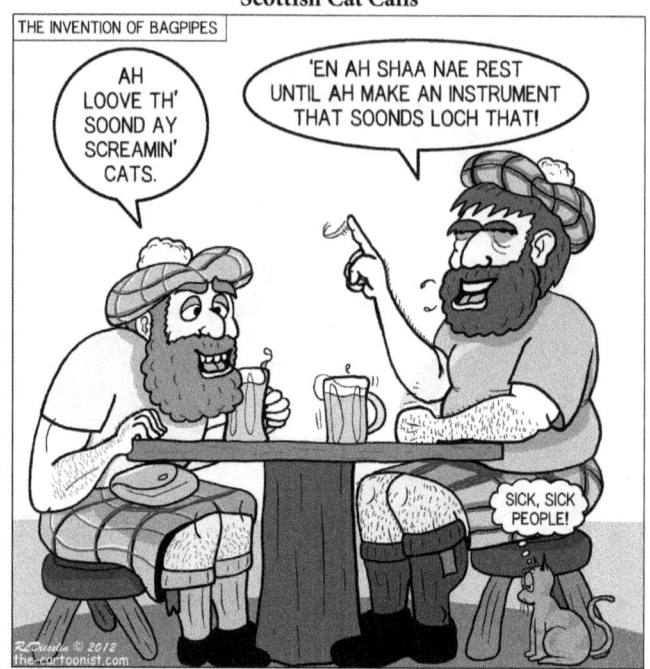

Cat Owner Ultimatum

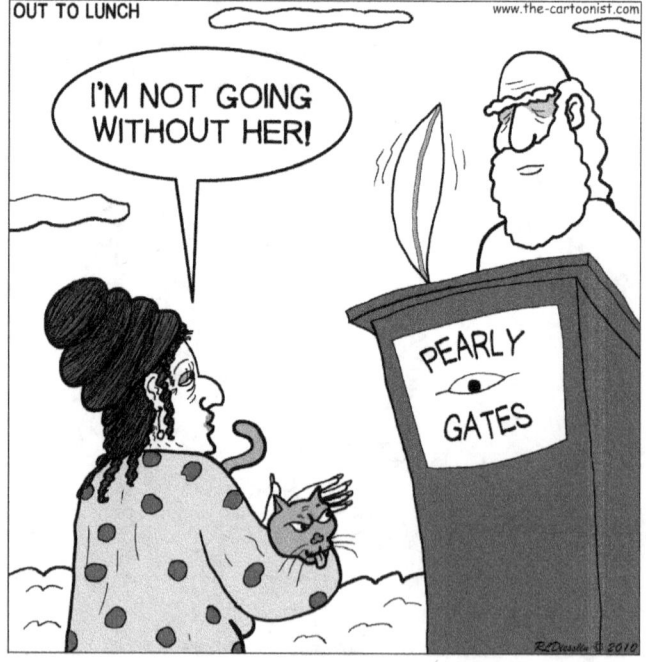

Cat Hibernation

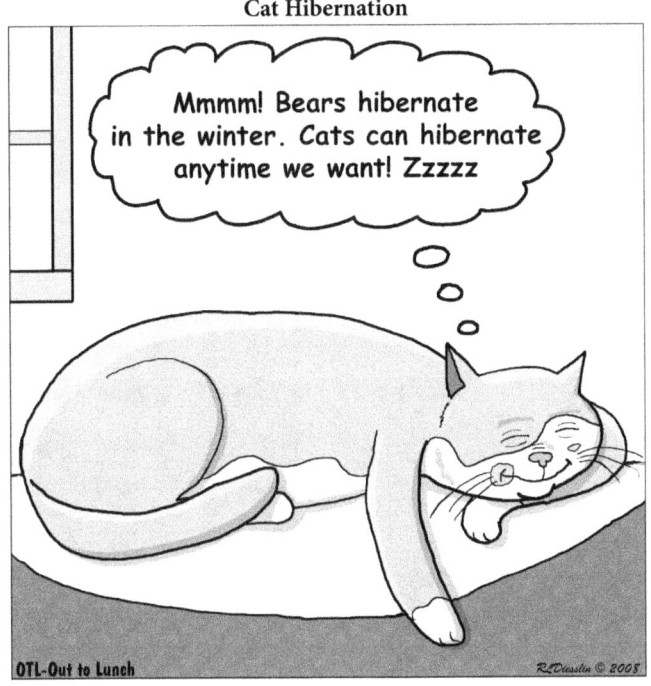

Privacy Issues

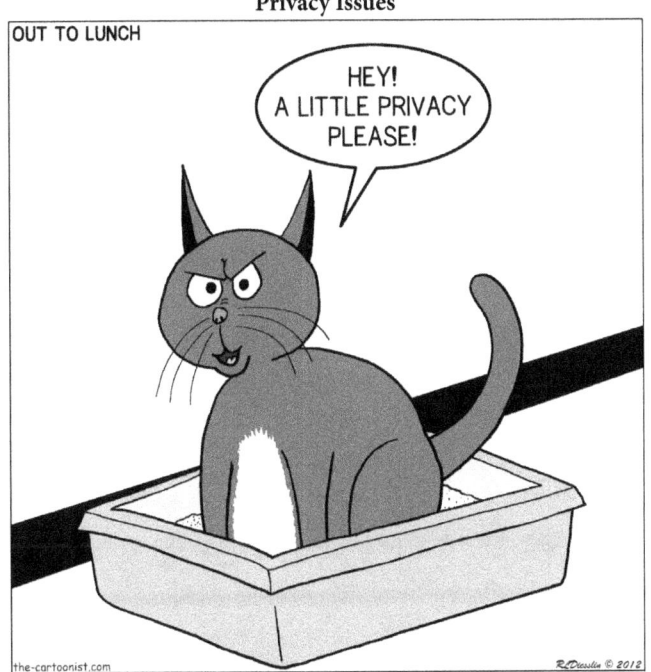

Sunshine On My Shoulders

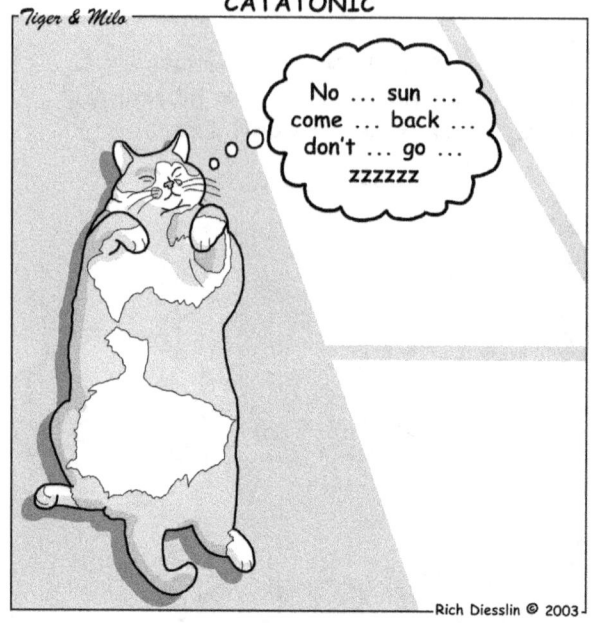

Cow Winter Olympics

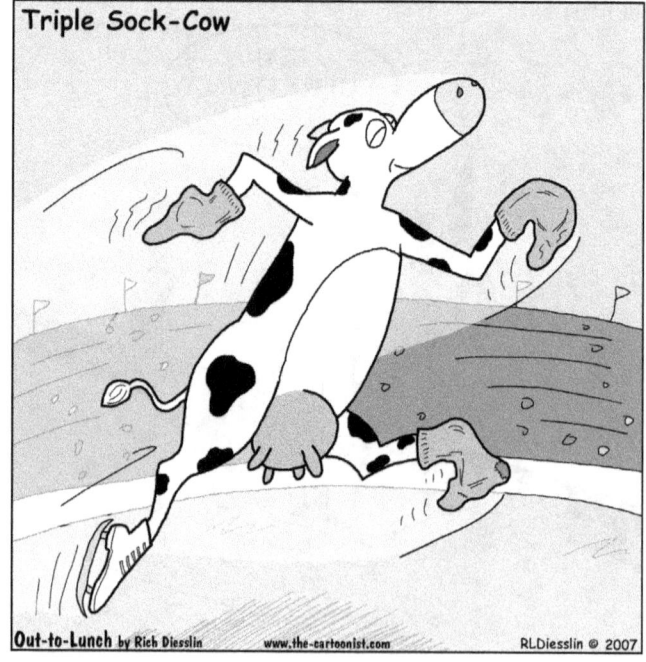

McBessie's

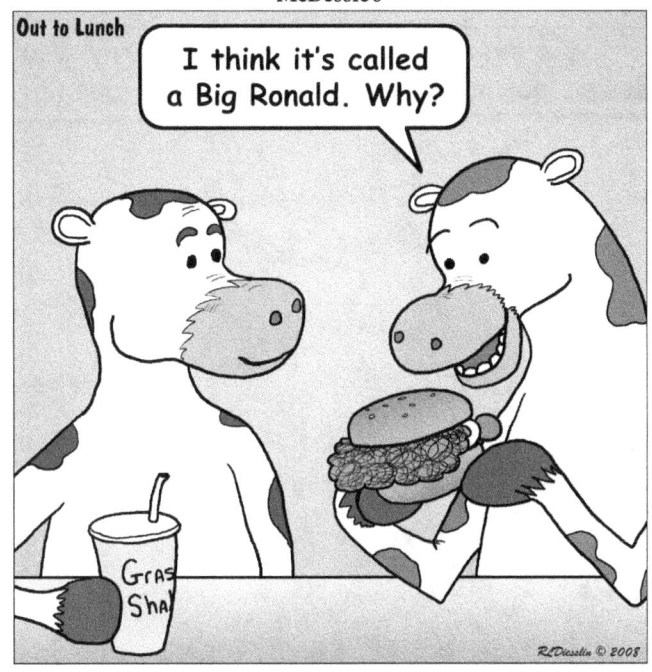

Bull

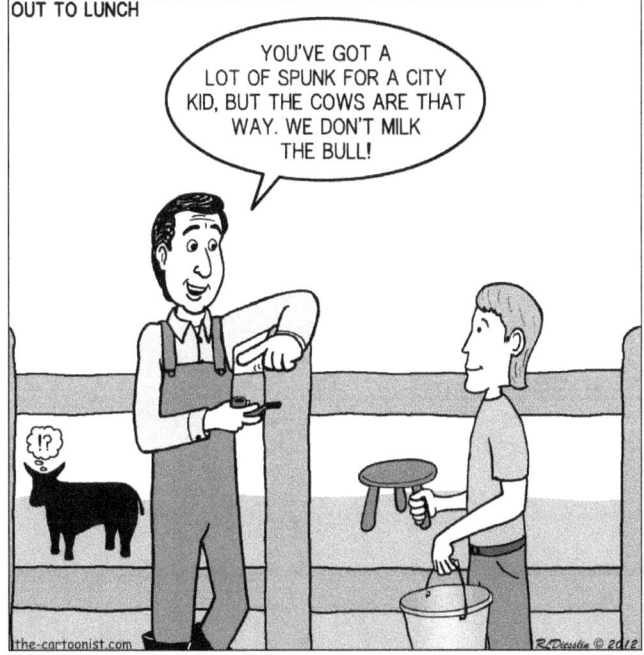

Cow Pies

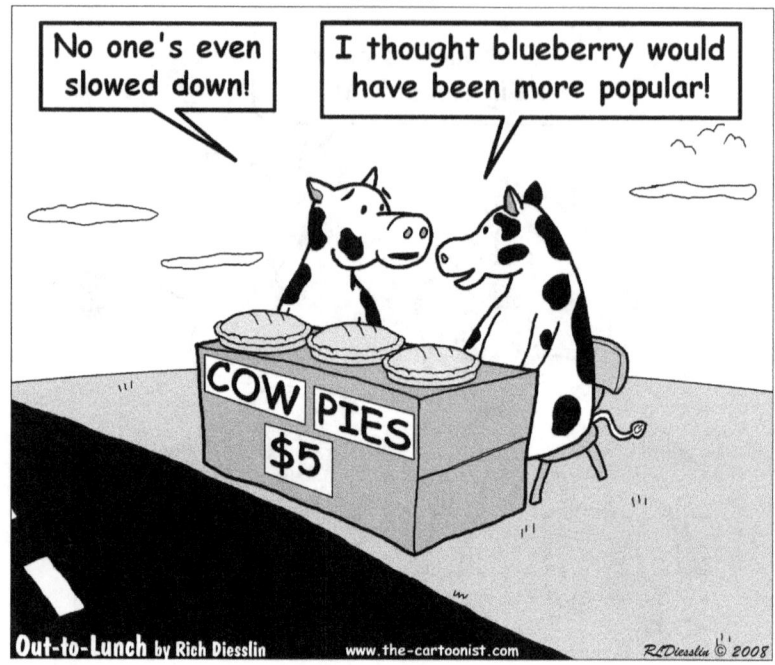

Left Hoof Yellow

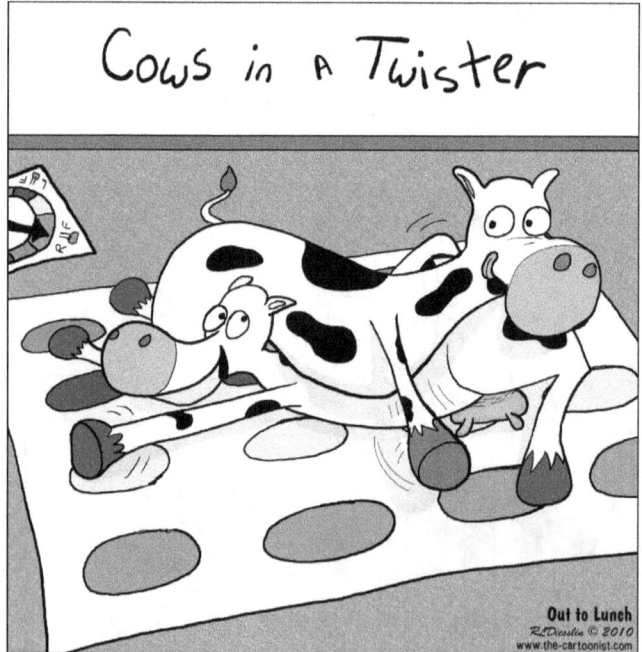

Favorite Crocodile Songs

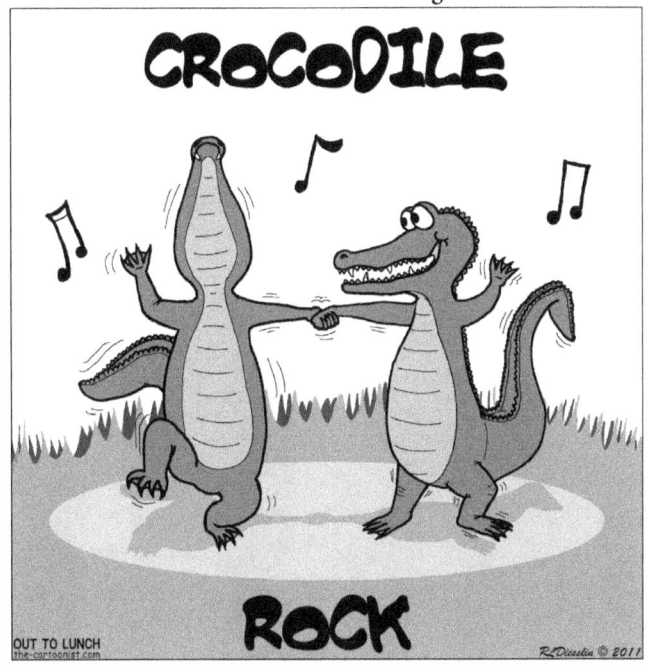

Alligator Dinner Plans

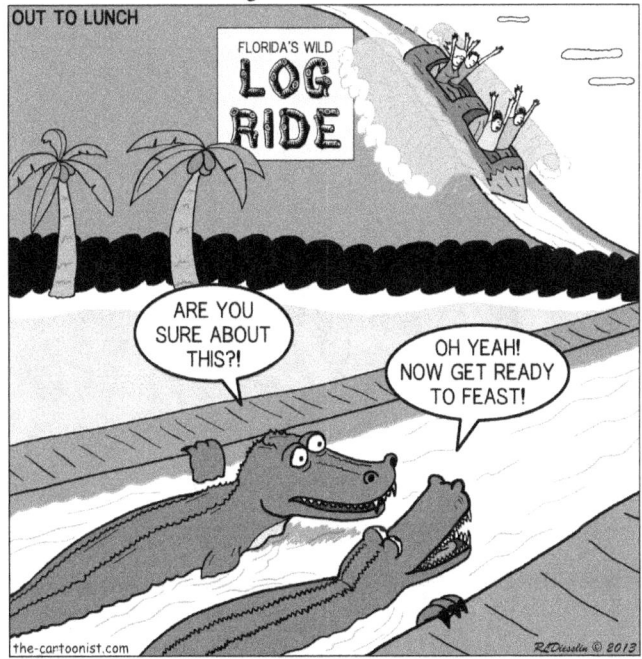

Dogs and Dragons

Don't Let's Be Silly Now

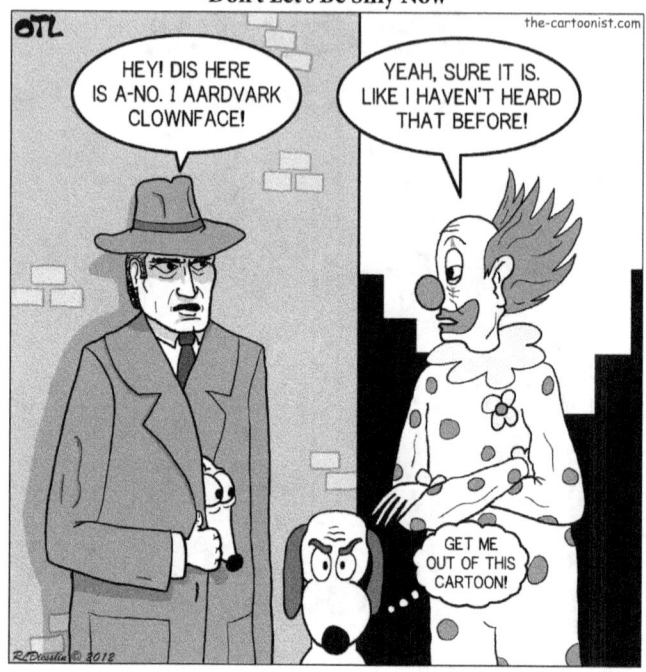

Discount Airlines

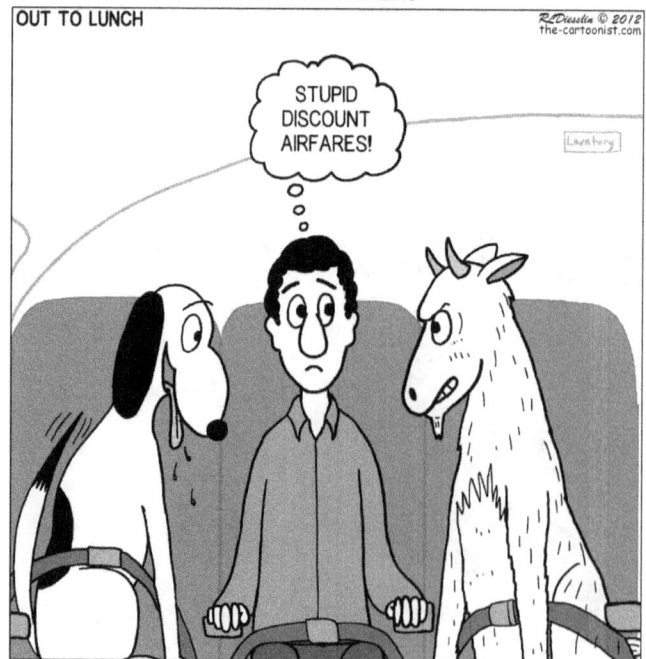

Answering Machine

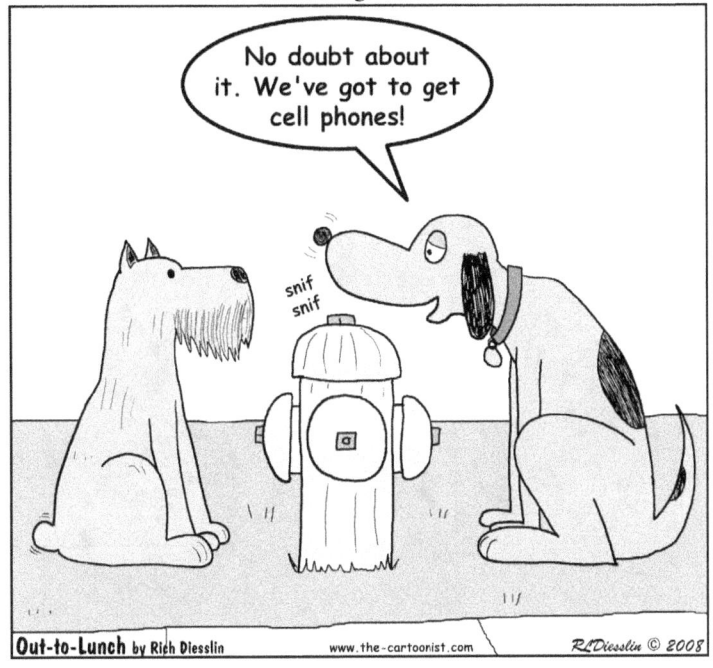

Lassie to the Rescue

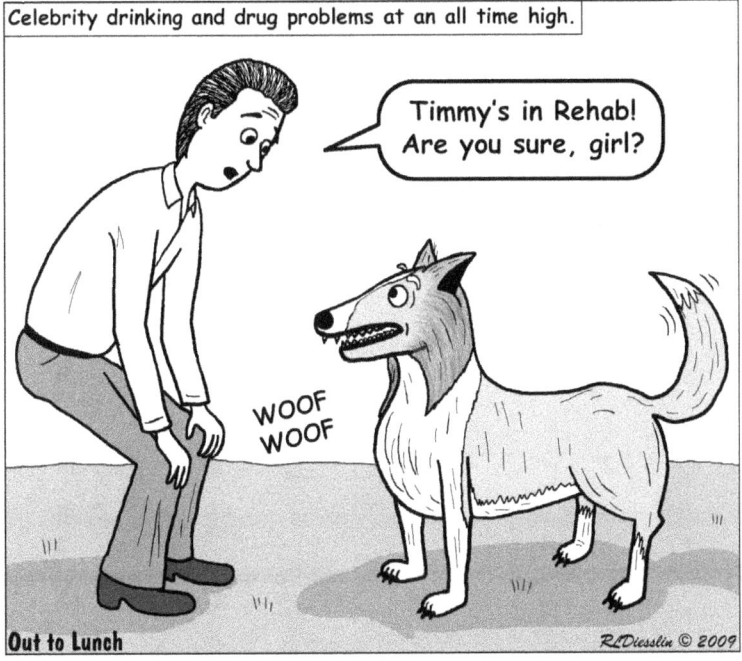

Doggy Tricks

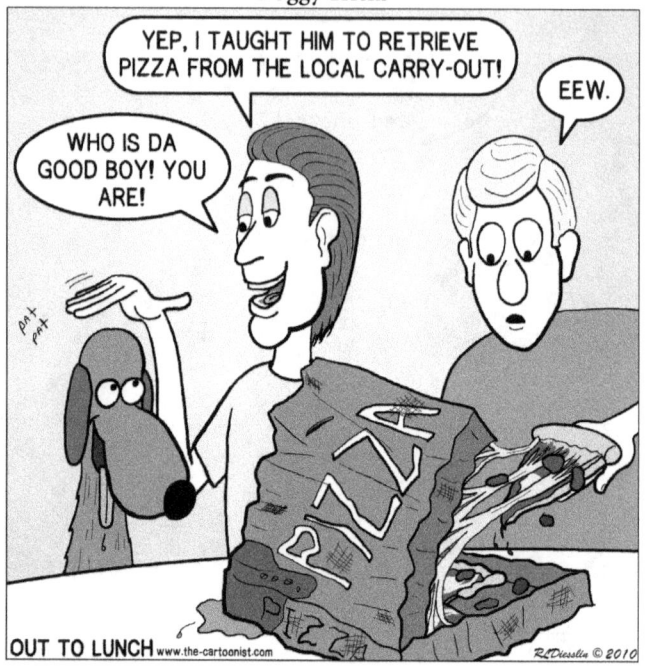

Putting on the Ritz

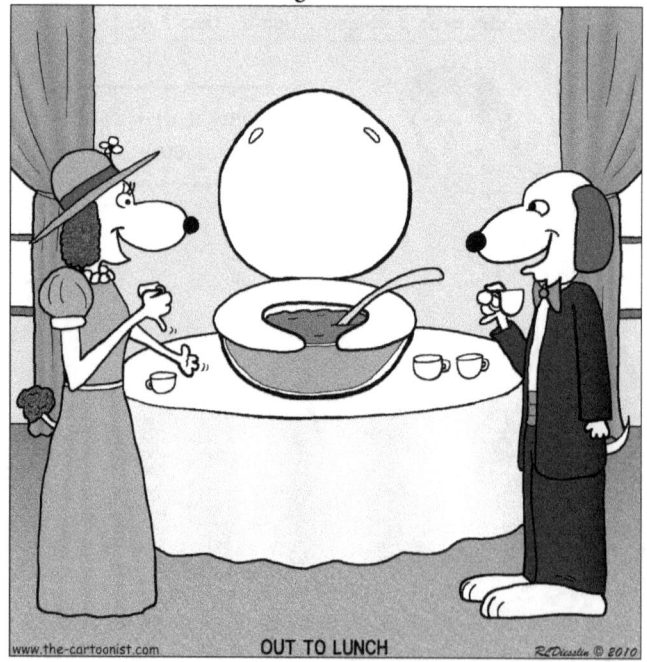

Out to Lunch - Dogs and Dragons - 22

Fox and Hound

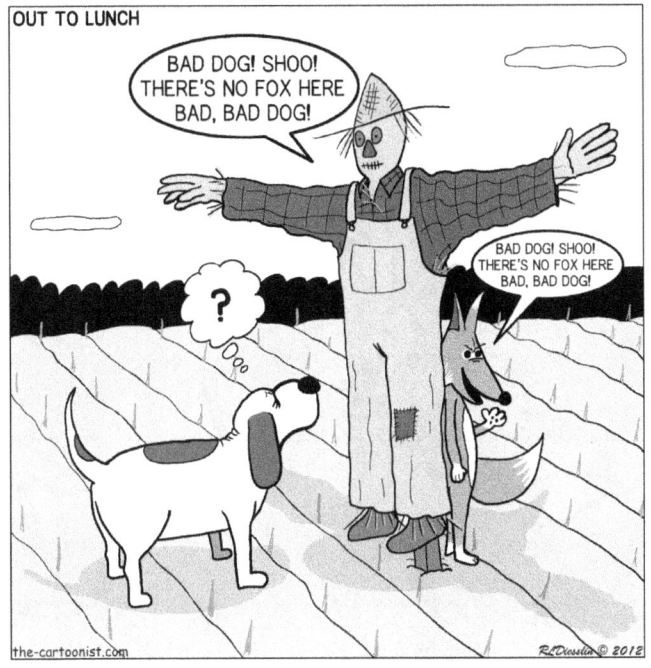

Questionable Practices

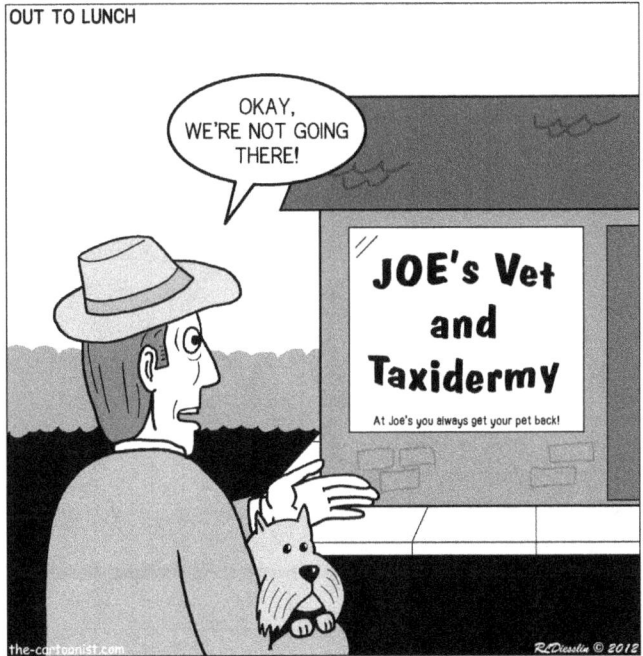

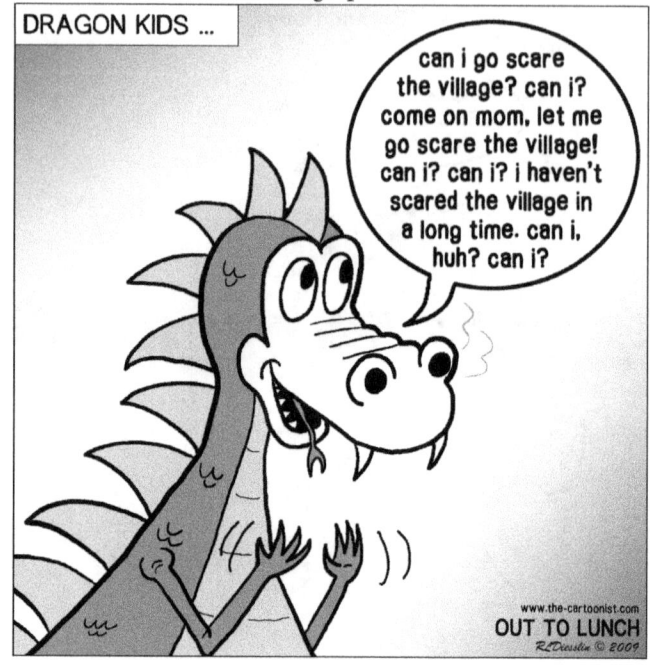

Eagles, Eels and Elephants

Bald Eagle Issues

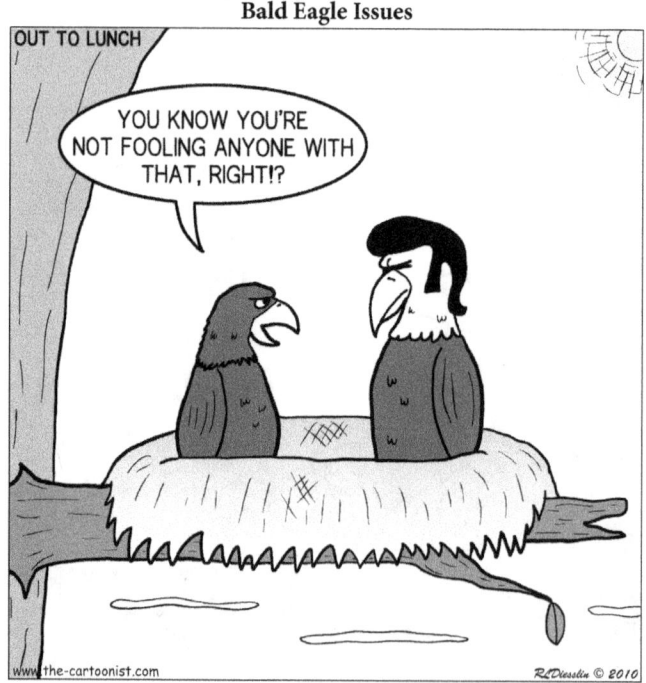

Famous Entertainers

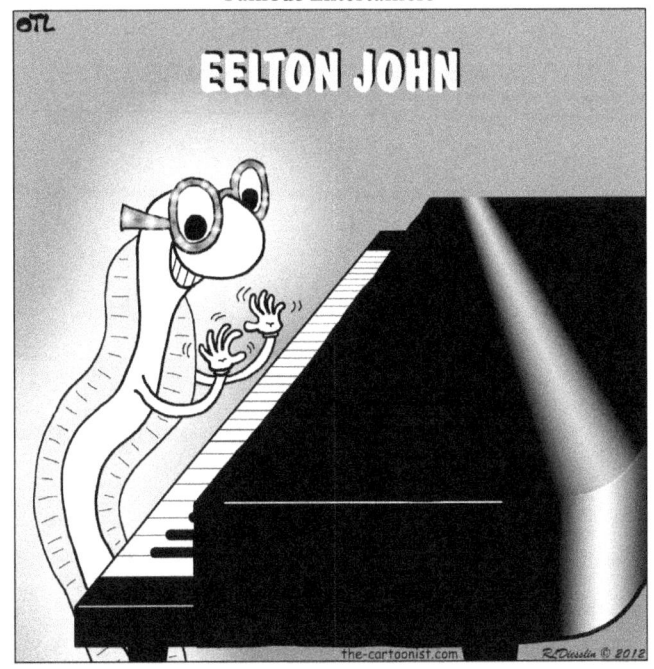

Elephant PC Phobias

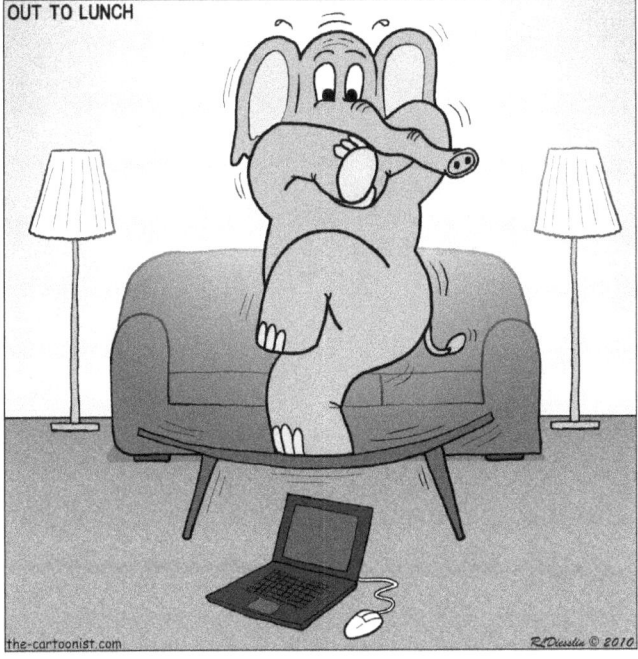

Fish and Frogs

Technical Evolution

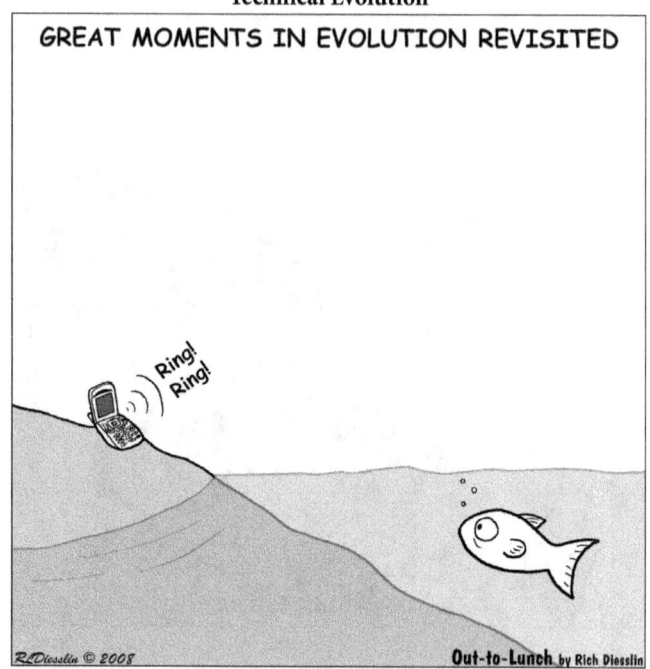

Fish Theology

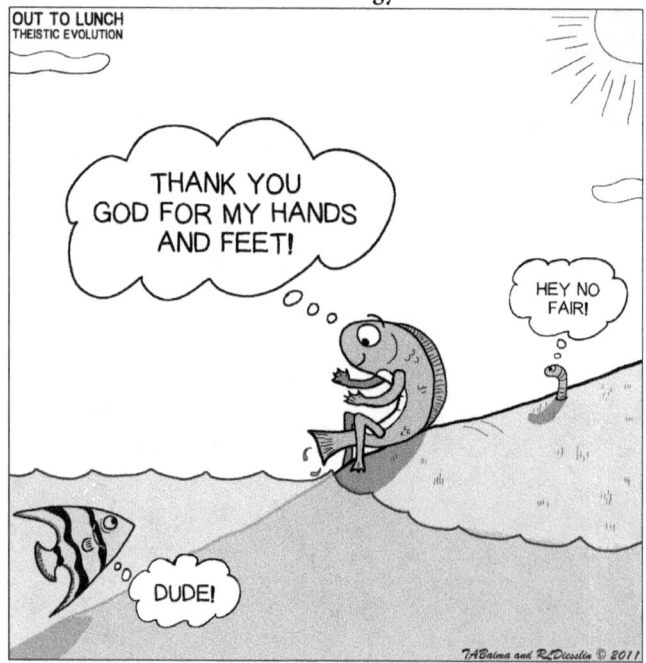

School of Fish

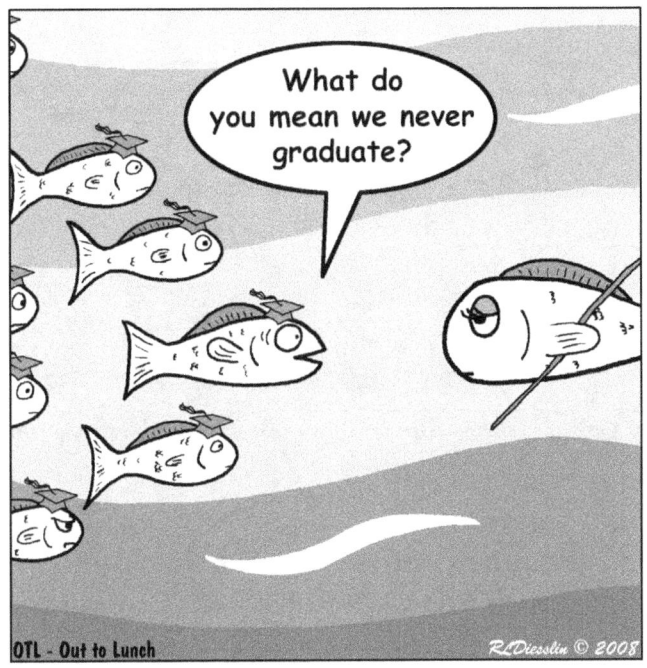

Spawning Season

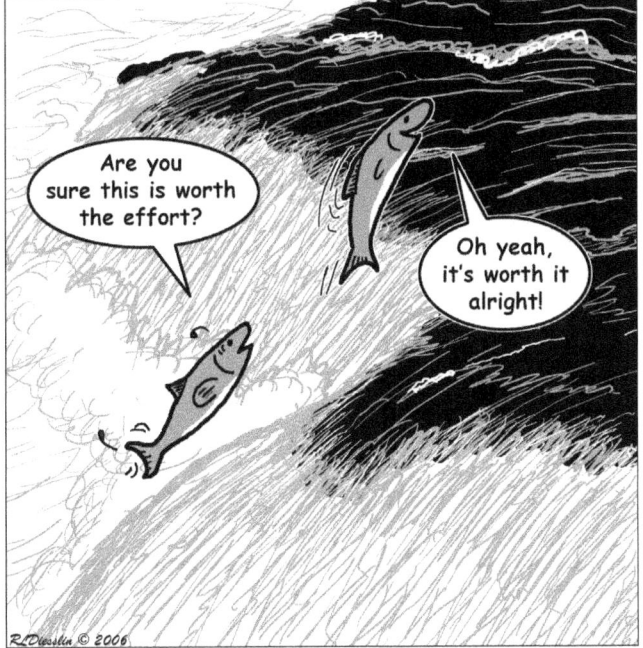

Fish Quandaries

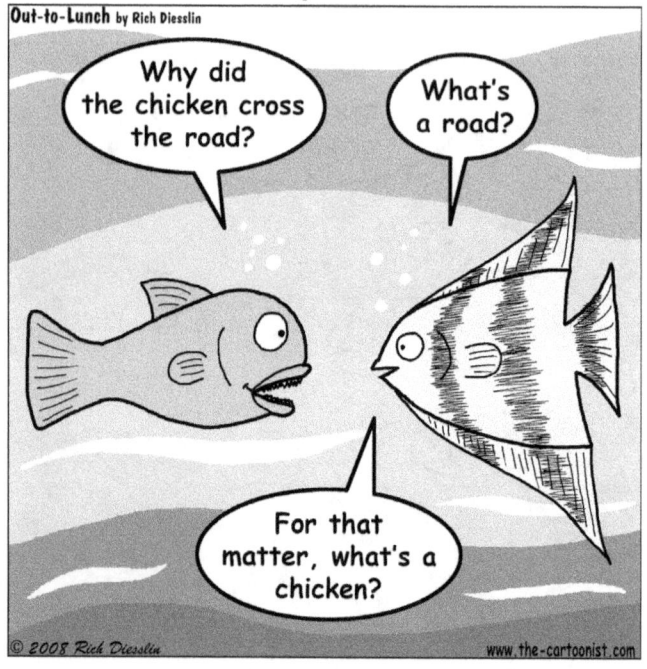

Clown Fish

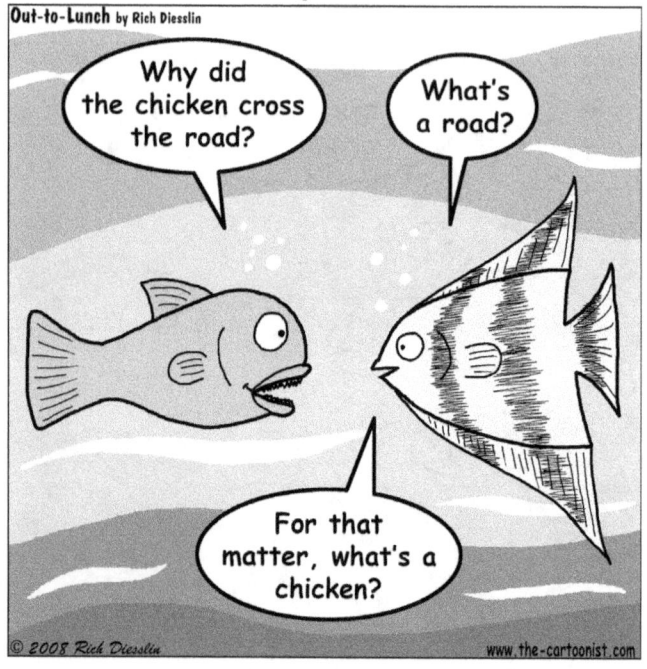

Out to Lunch - Fish and Frogs - 28

Fresh Fish

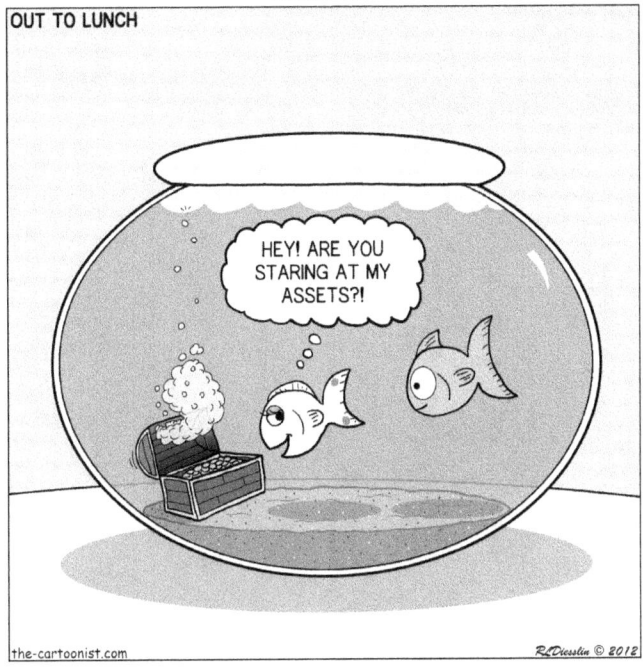

Fishing for Answers

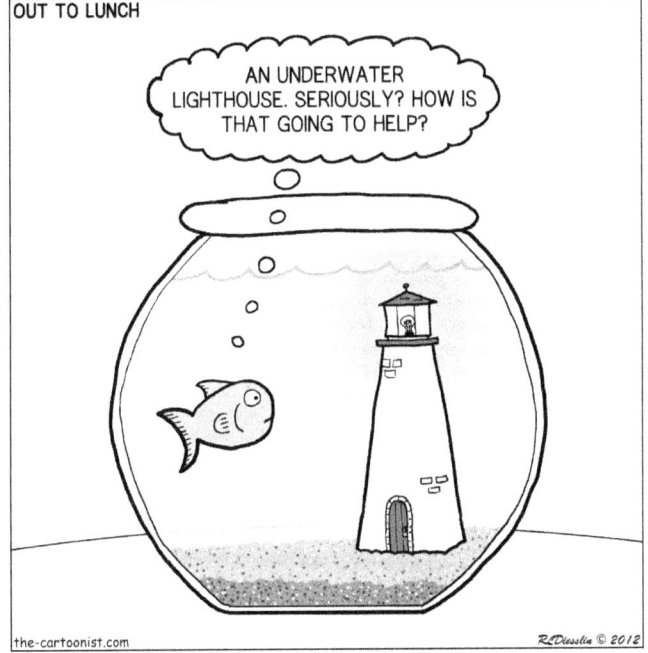

Fishbowl Games

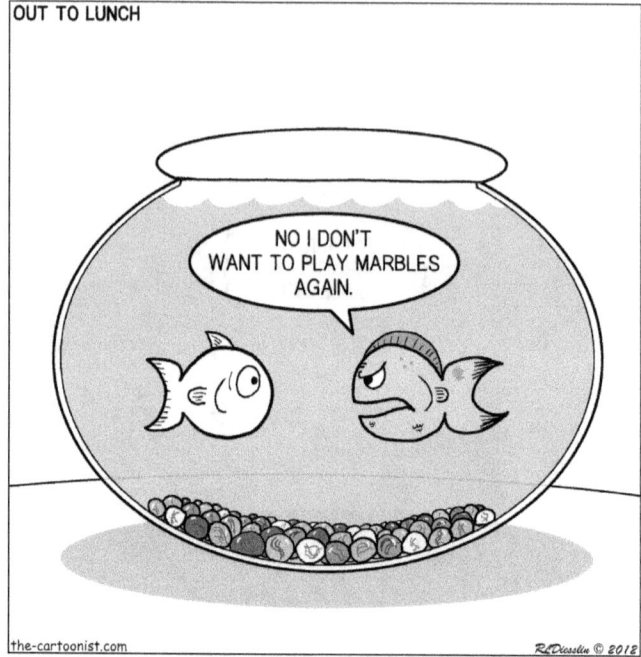

Really Fresh Fish

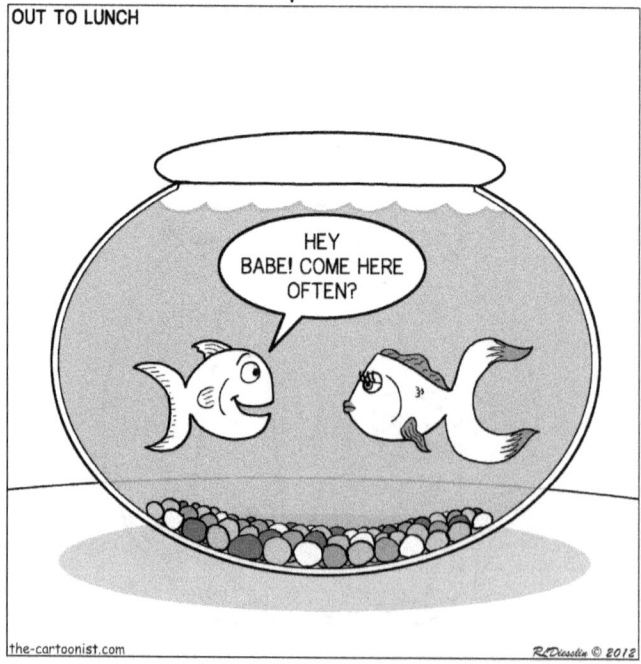

Goldfish

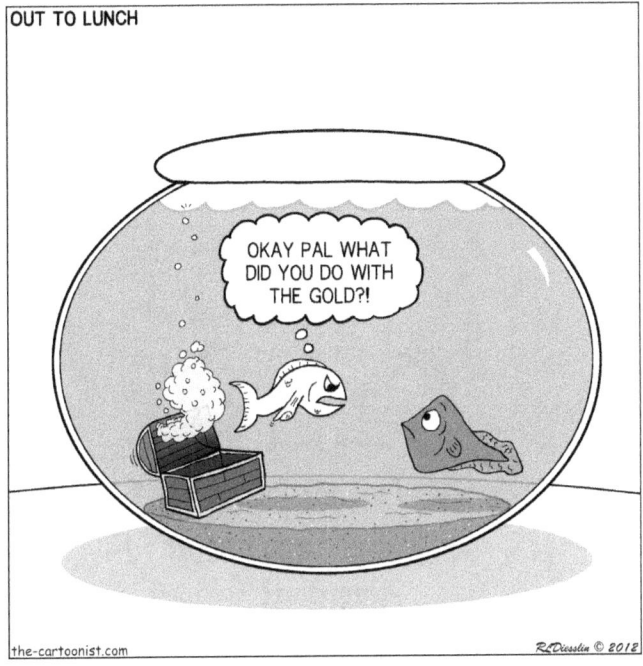

Treasure Chest

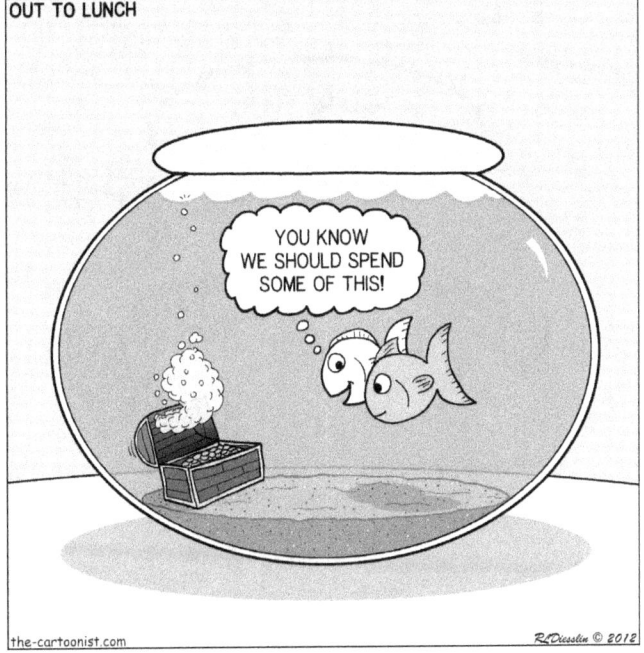

Fish Food

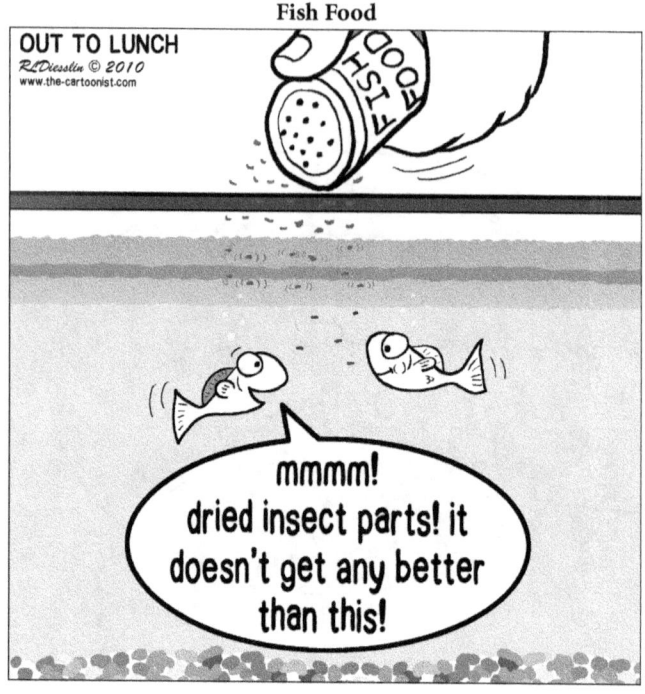

Fish Mother's Day

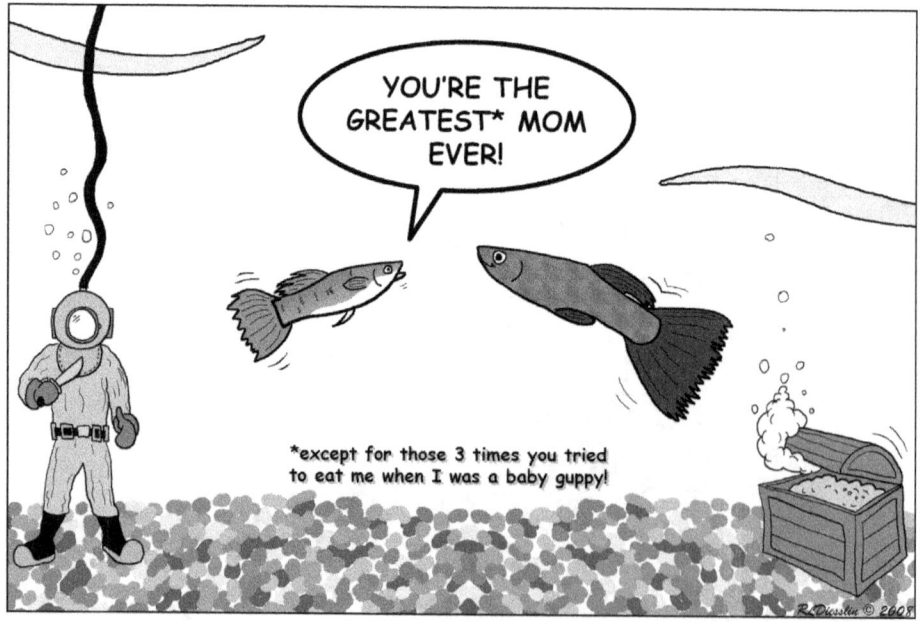

Diver Dan

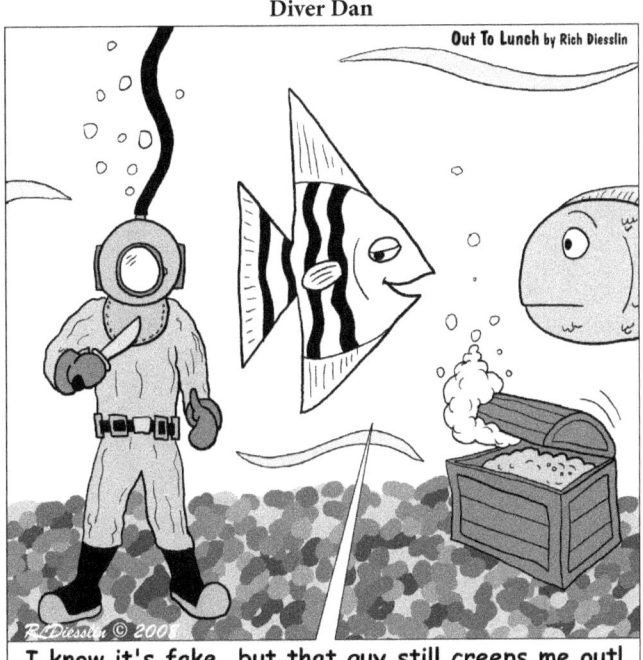

Horsing Around

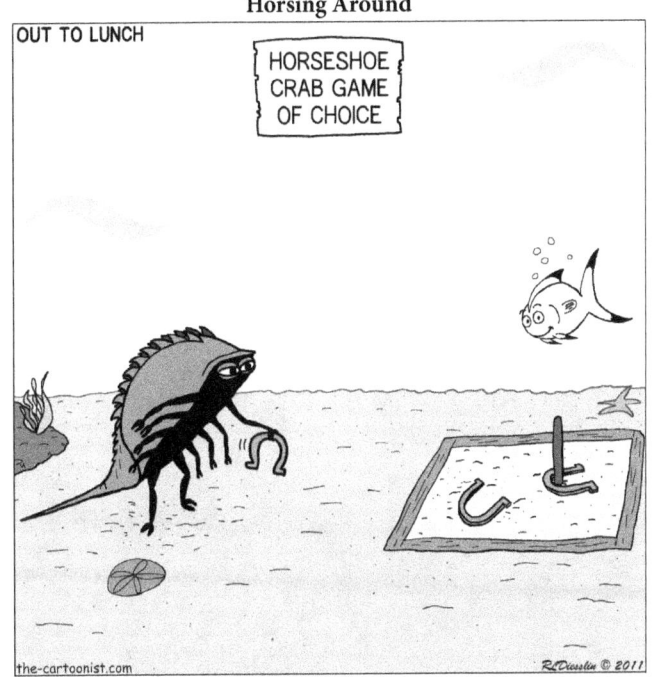

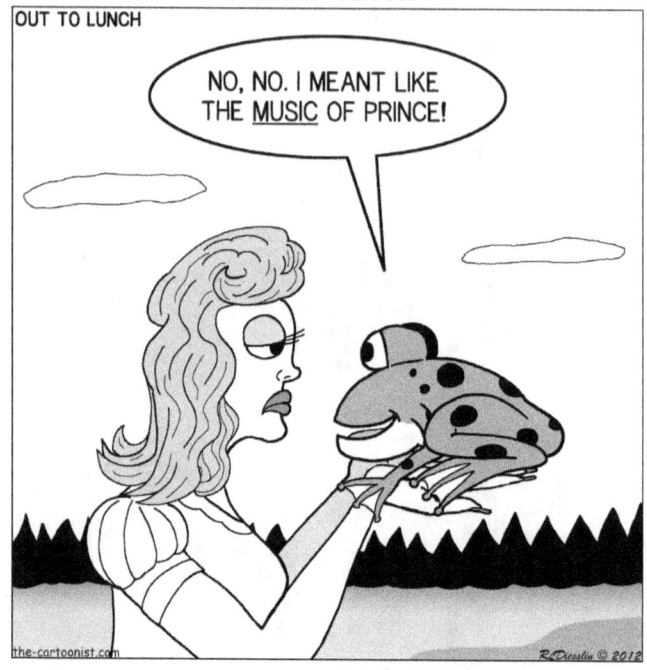

Geckos, Geese, Giraffes and Gorillas

Geckos Gone Wild

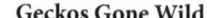

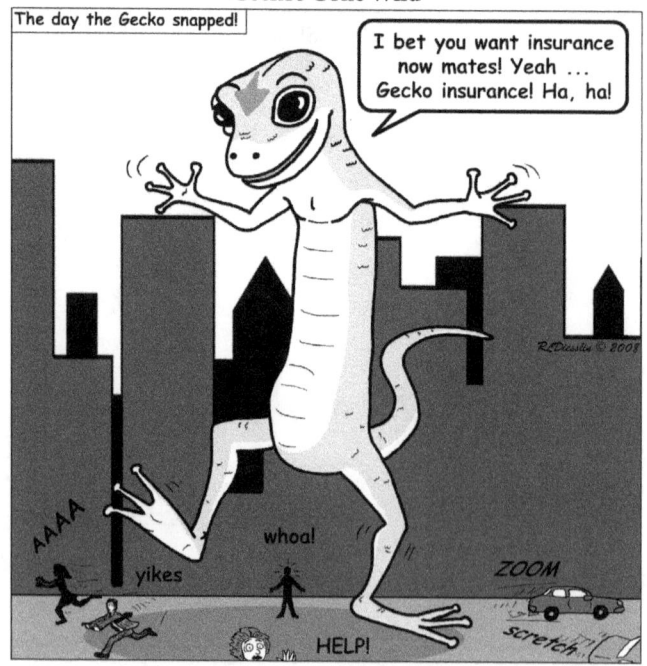

Goose Problems

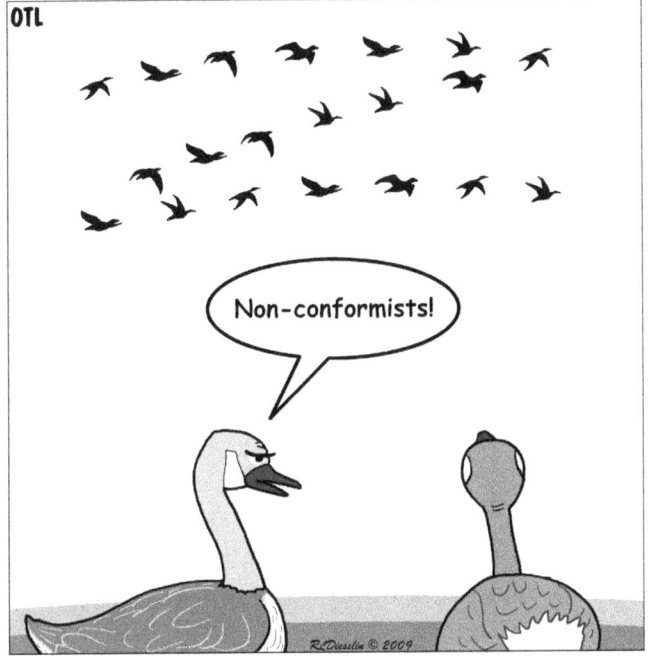

Faulty Towers

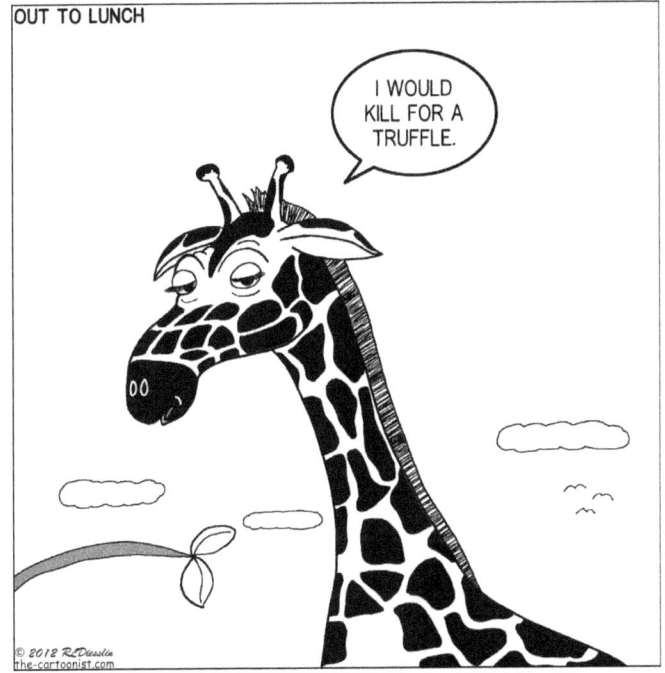

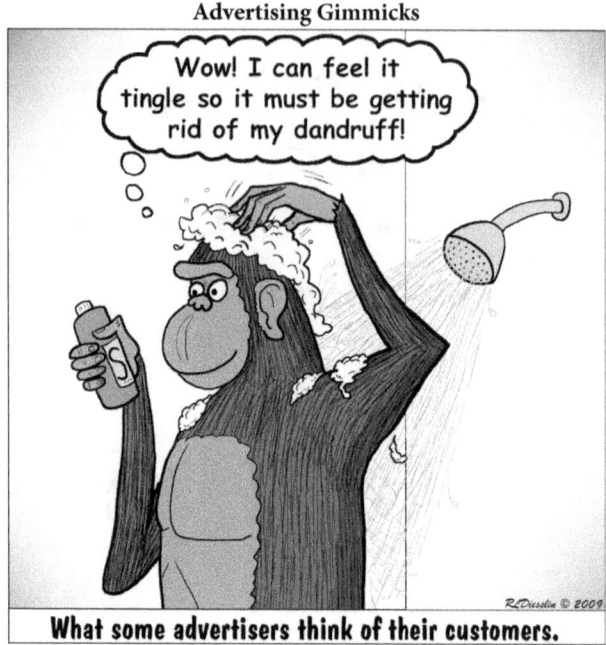

What some advertisers think of their customers.

Bonus: Selected KNOTS Animal Cartoons

We interrupt these OTL cartoons to bring you some animal-related Knots or Not Scout cartoons for your viewing pleasure.

KNOTS cartoons involve all kinds of scout situations, many of which are outdoor activities and can often include animals. KNOTS cartoons have appeared monthly on the website of the U.S. Scouting Service Project, my web site (www.the-cartoonist.com) and in the daily newspaper of the Boy Scouts of America National Jamboree, and elsewhere.

The original KNOTS or Not concept was to have fun with silly situations that you would NOT do or find in scouting (sort of humorous opposites). Very quickly it evolved into a more general cartoon format ... sometimes "nots" and sometimes just silliness. Even so the name remains and is sometimes shortened to KNOTS. So, I hope you enjoy these selected KNOTS animal cartoons!

Taking it to a New Level

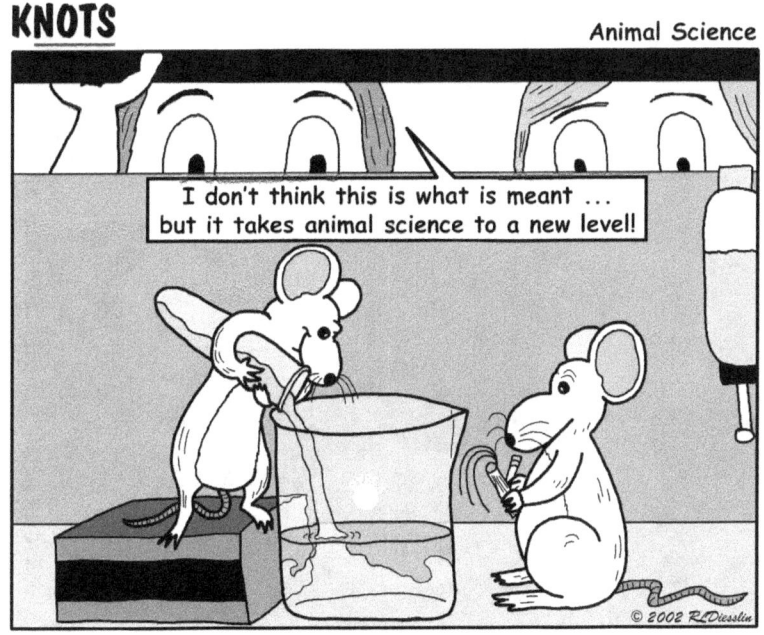

Ant Farm?

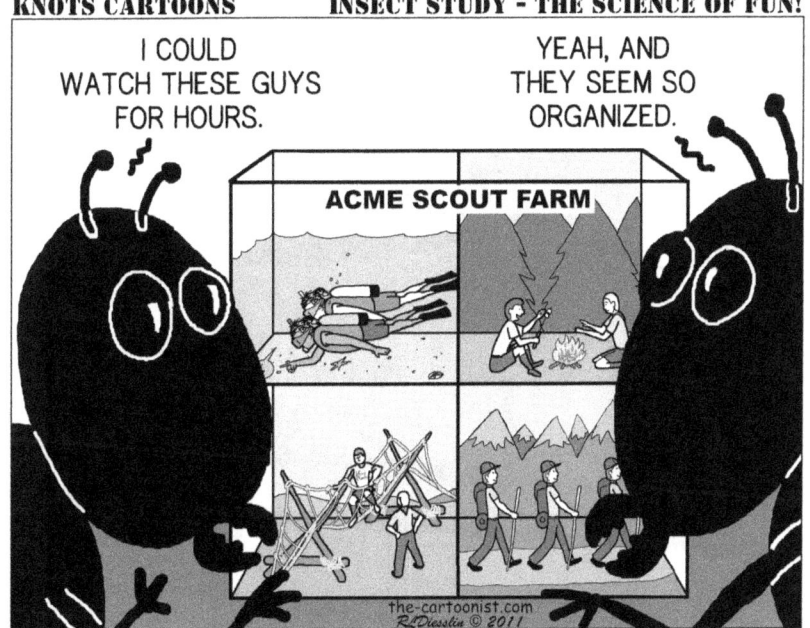

Bat Study

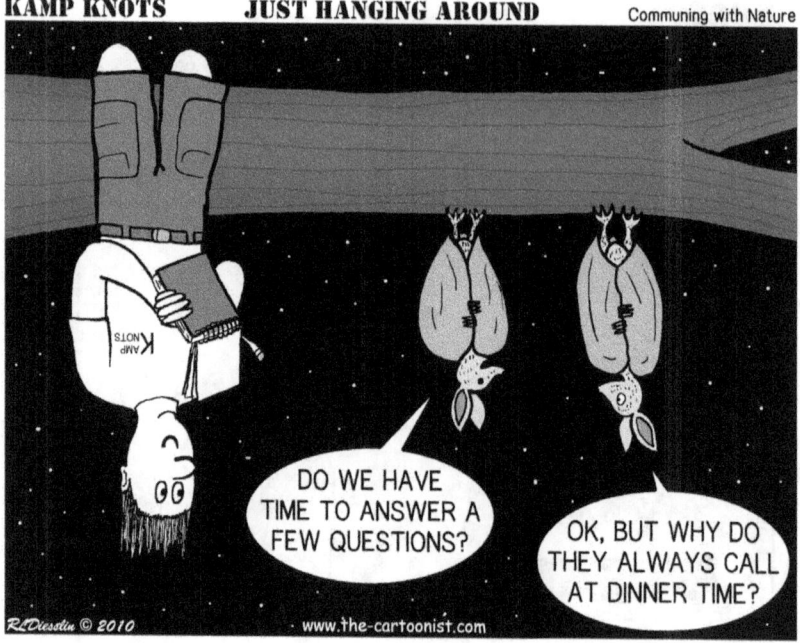

Runaround

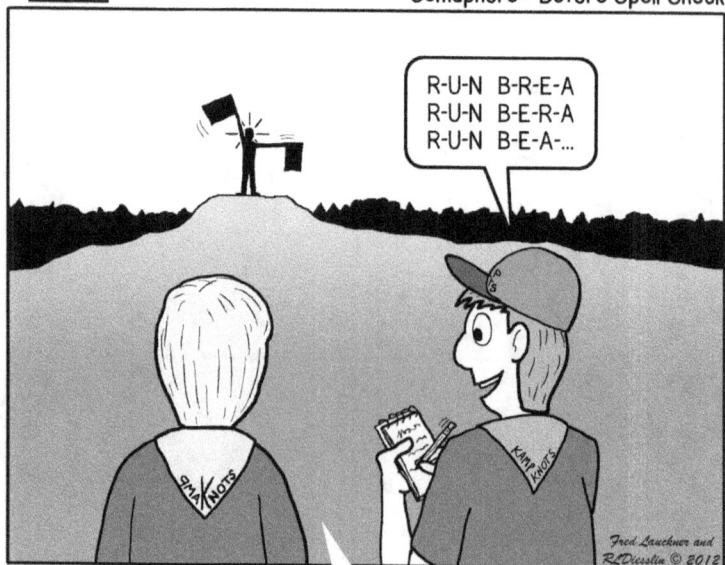

KNOTS   **WATCH THE BIRDIE**   Bird Study Merit Badge

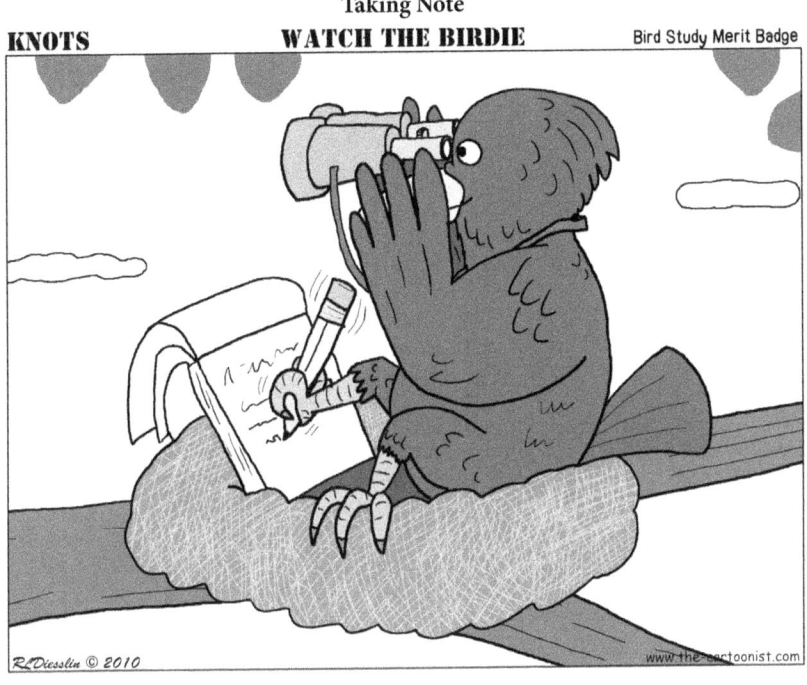

No Fly Zone

KNOTS   **USE A GOOD CHECKLIST**   Bugs

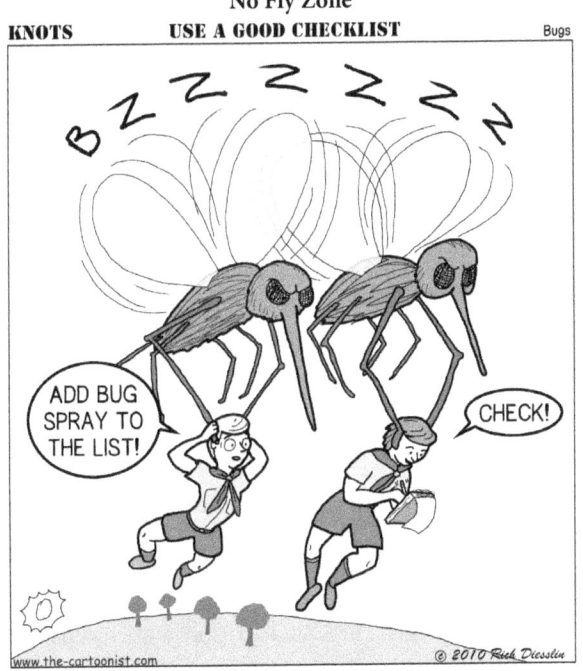

Deliverance

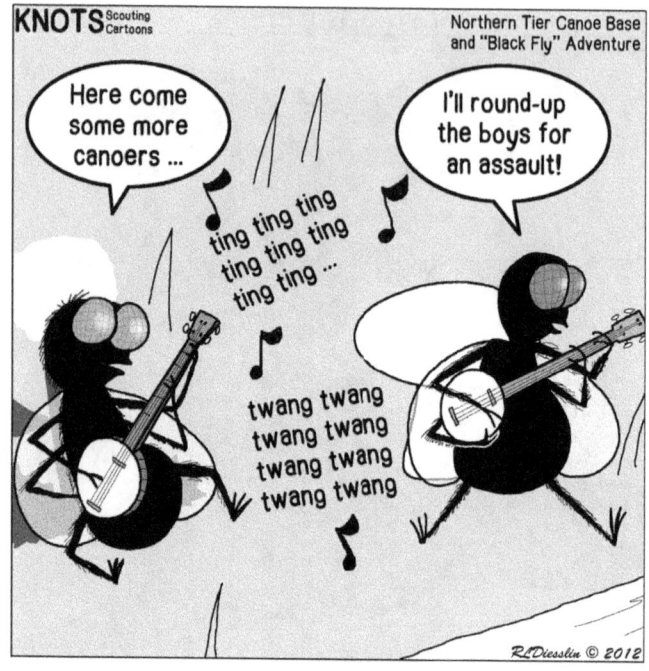

What's Up Doc?

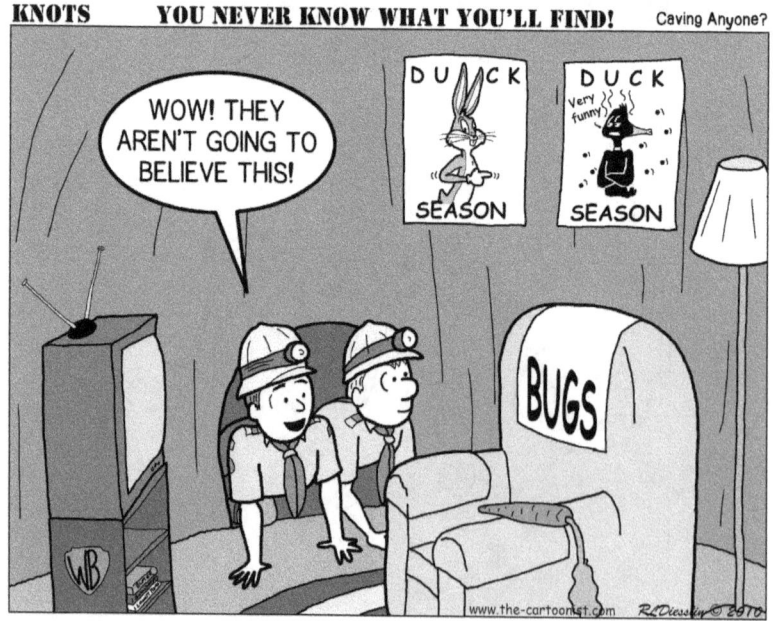

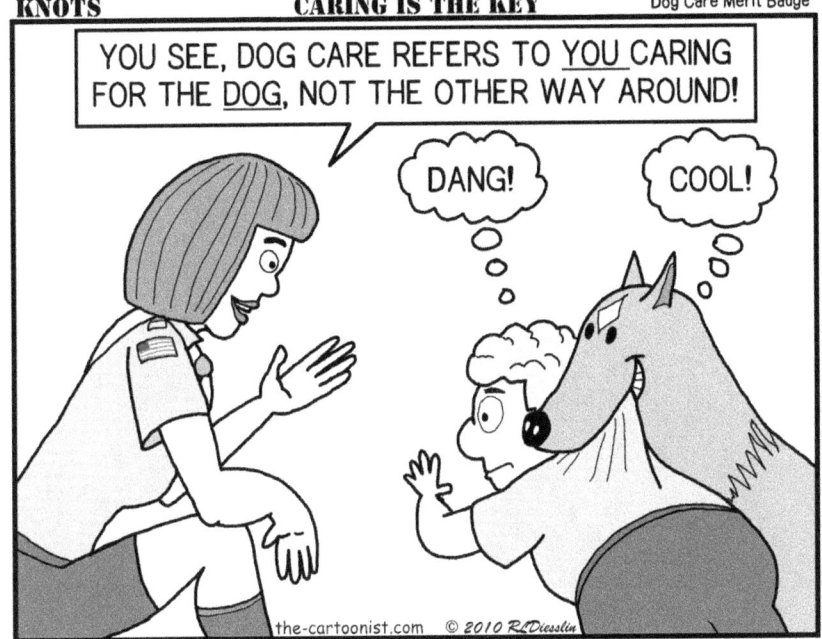

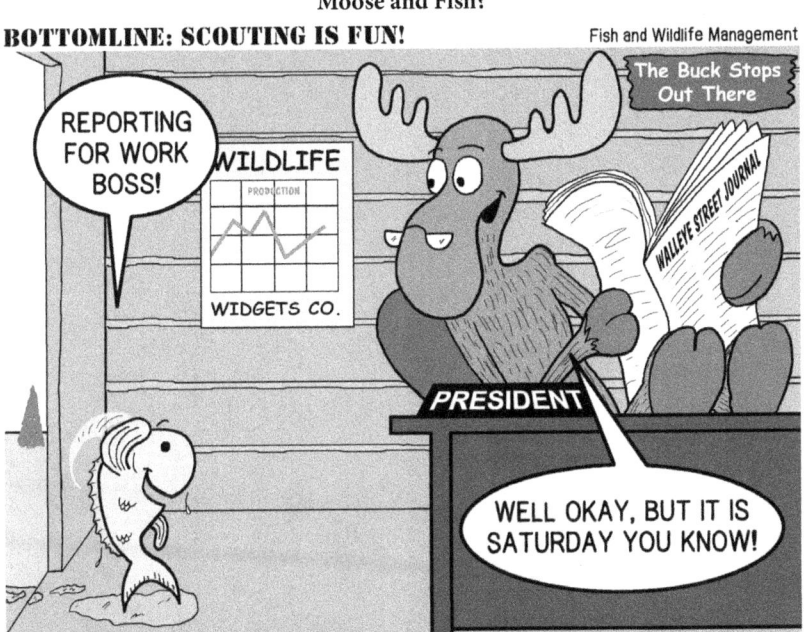

Weather Rock Forecast

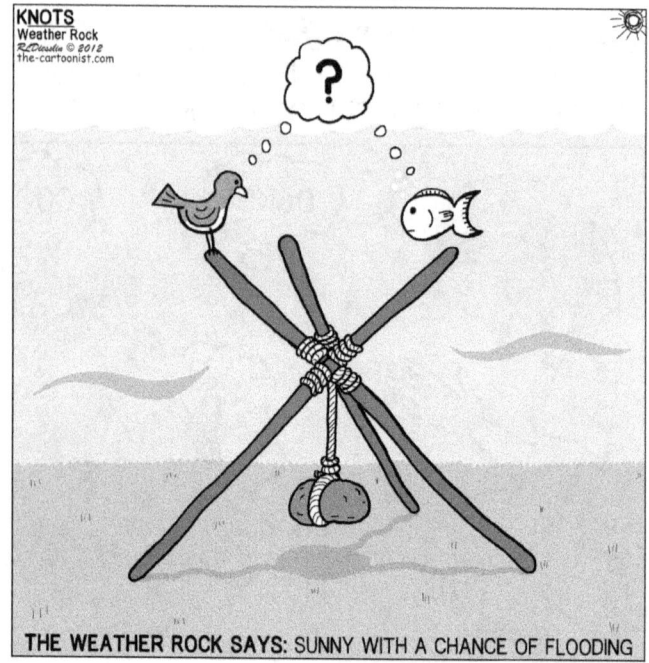

A Matter of Perspective

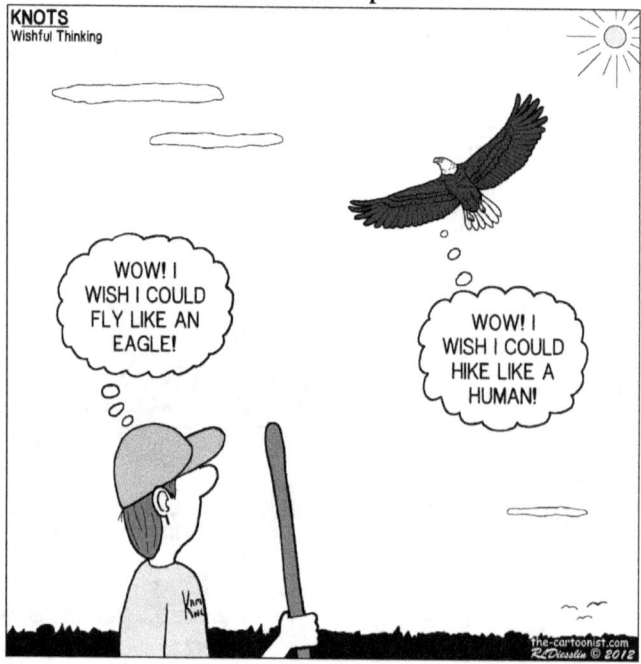

Swimming with the Jellyfishes

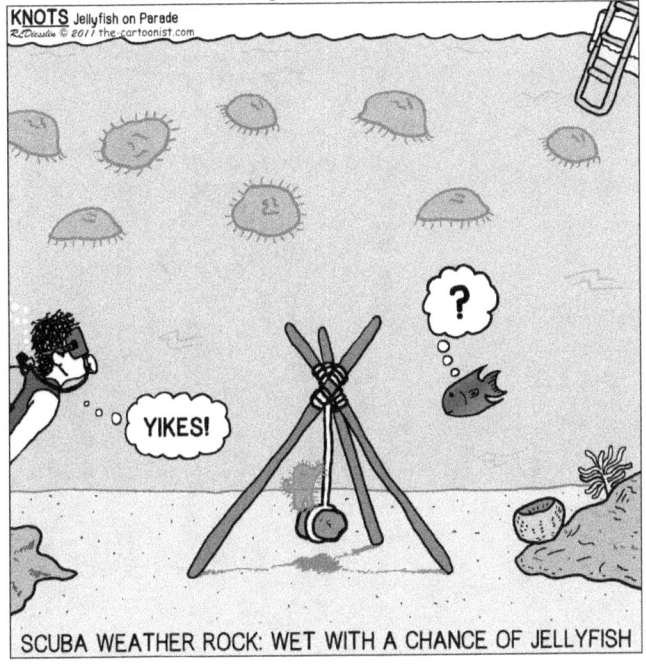

On Patrol

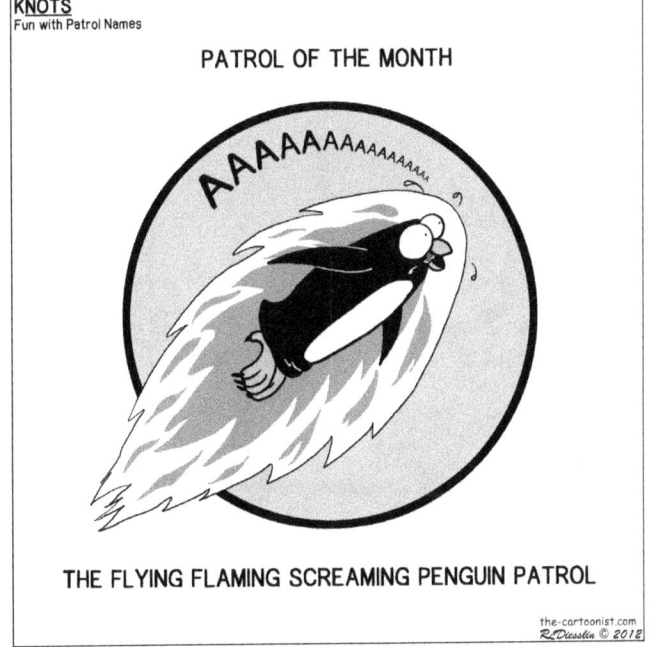

Animal Tales

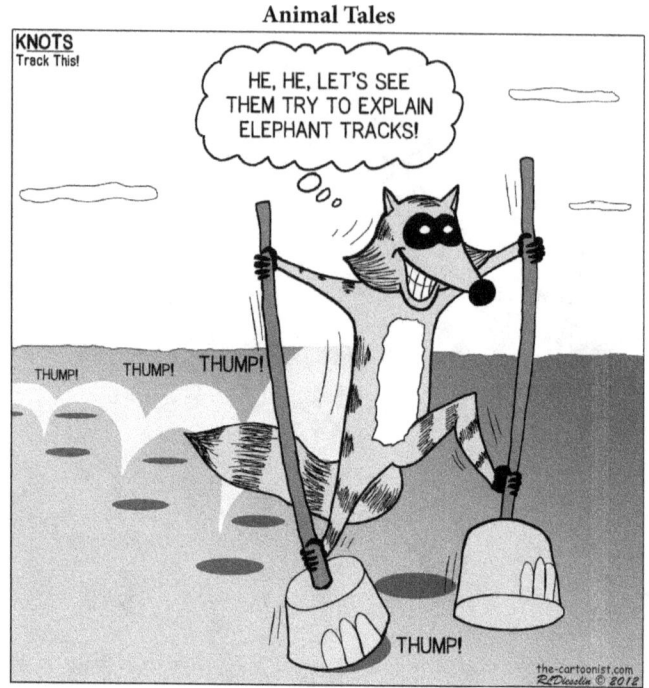

Pass the Popcorn

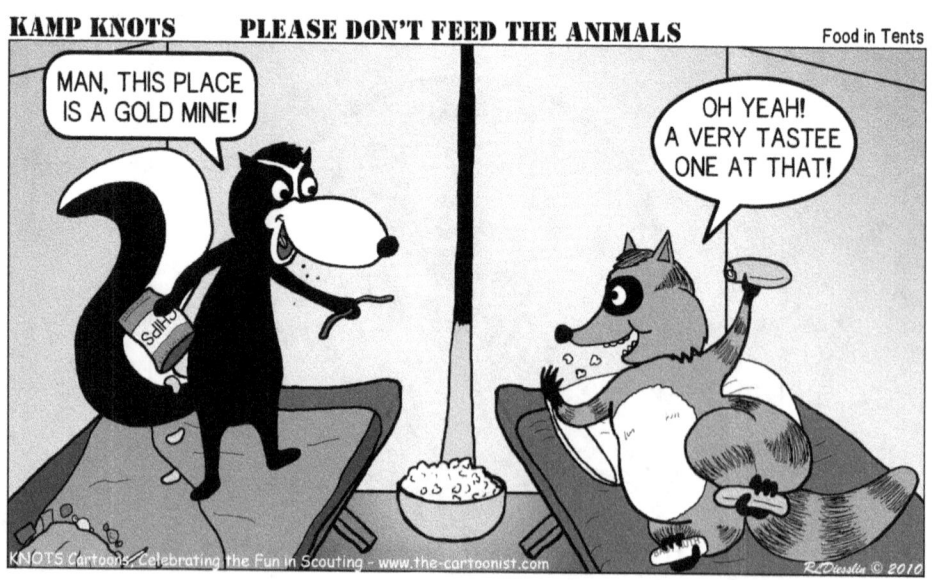

Turkey Time

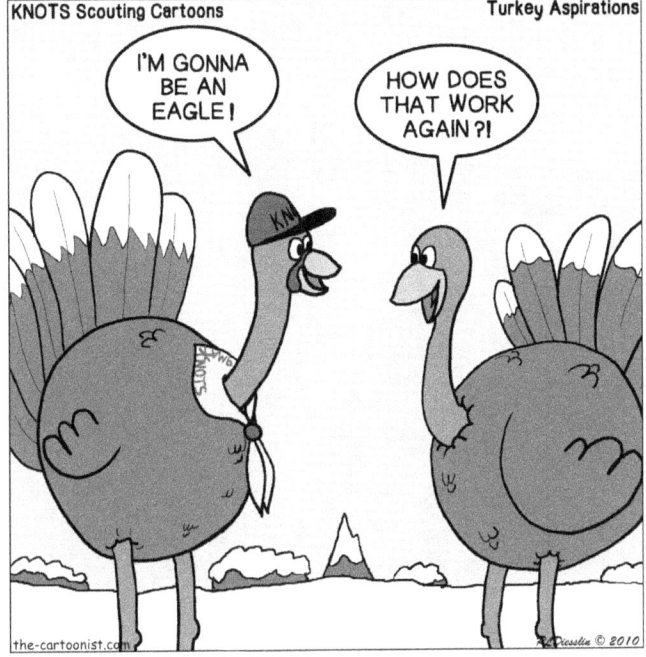

Take the Stroke

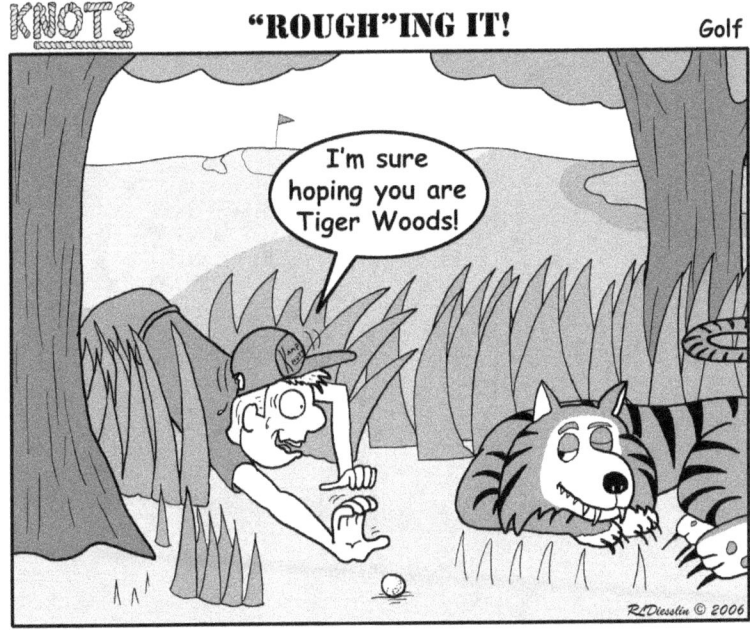

End of KNOTS Scout Cartoons! Now back to being Out to Lunch ...

Lions, Lobsters, and Manatees

Lioning Around

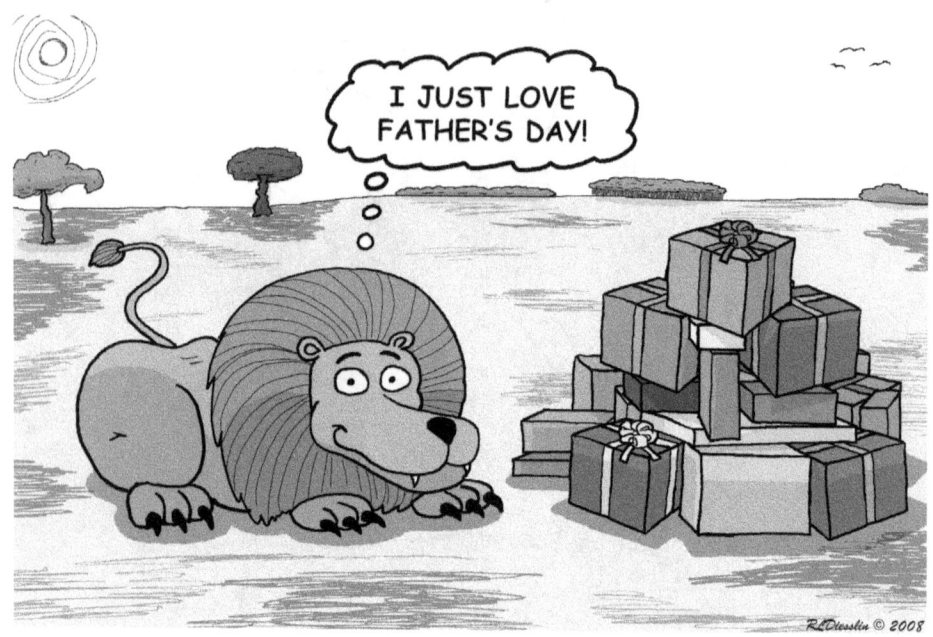

Sea Life Bragging Rights

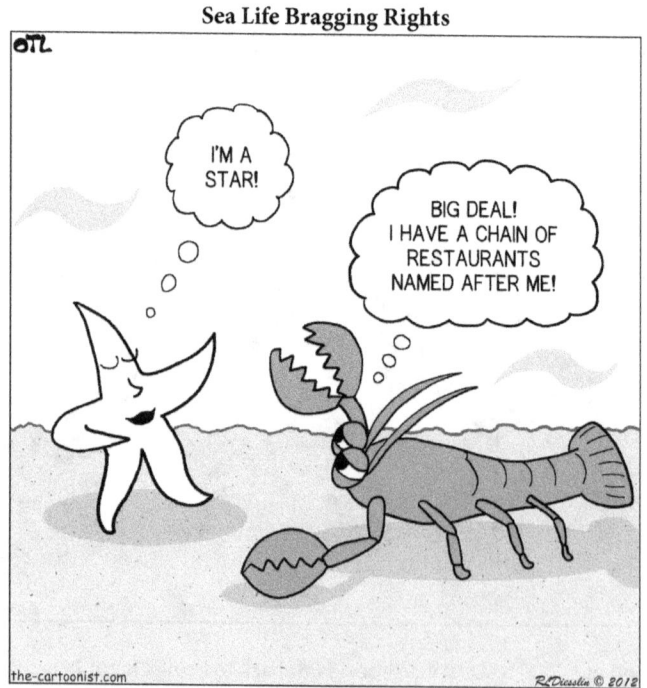

Not Exactly Club Med

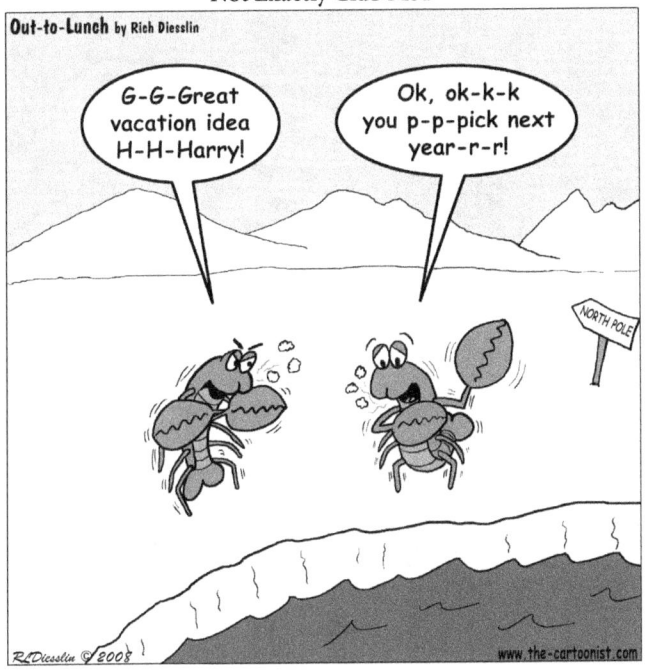

Not Exactly a Mermaid

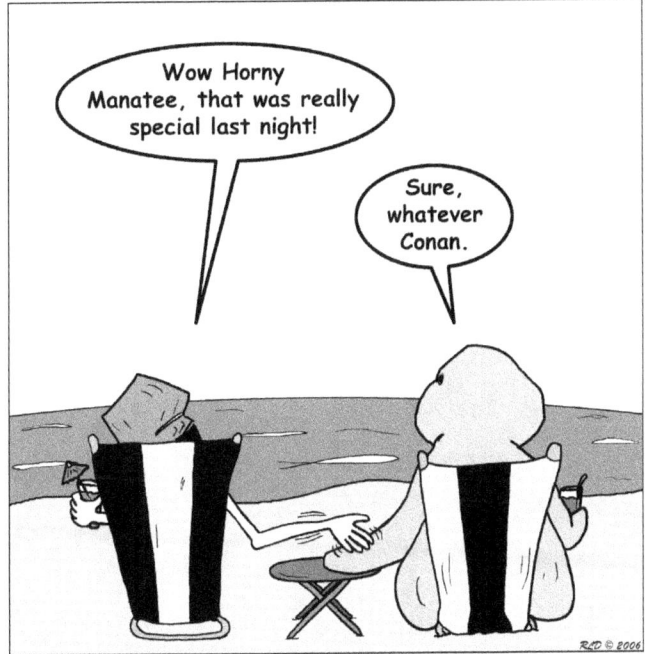

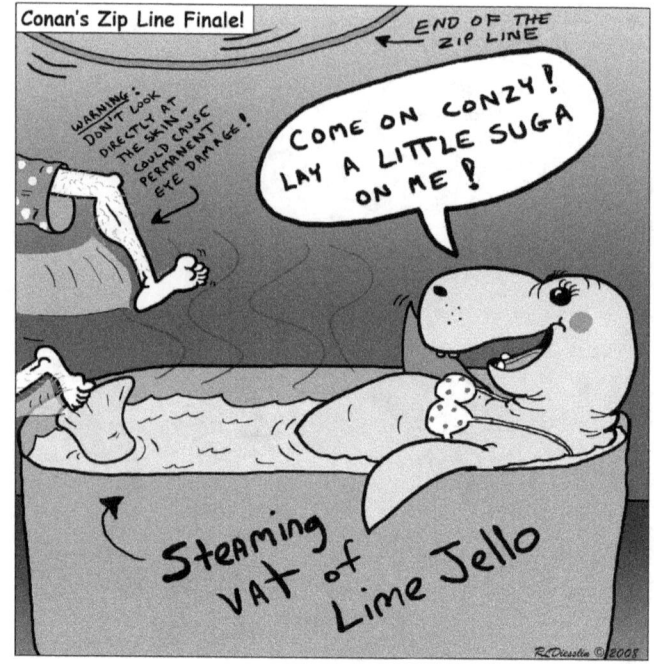

Mice and Monkeys

The Cartoon Sciences

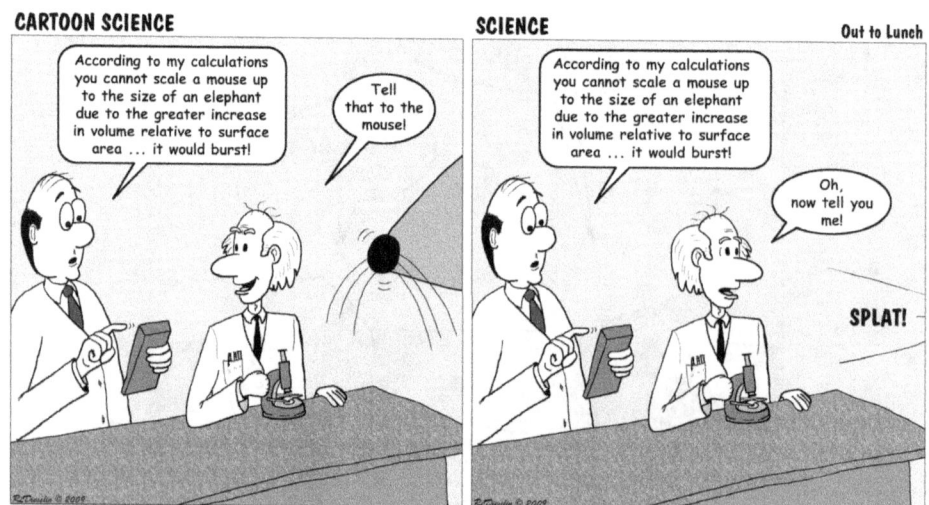

Only Your Hairdresser Knows for Sure

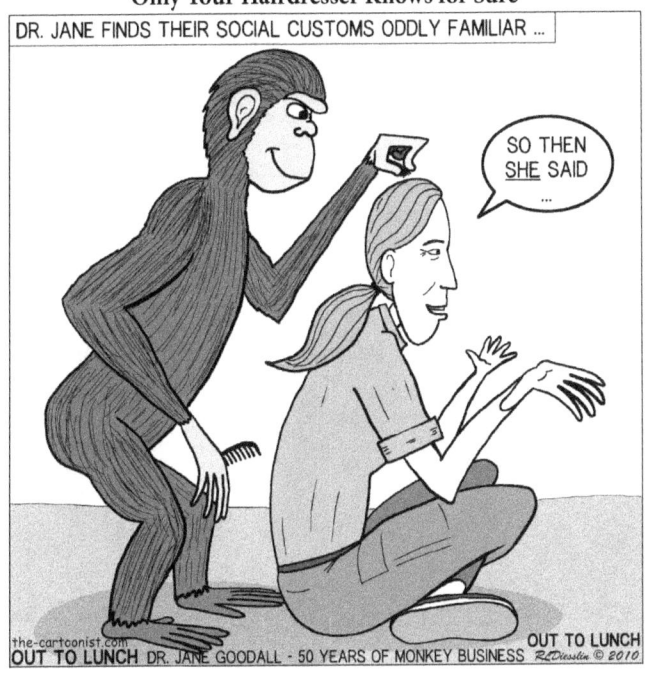

Monkey Manners

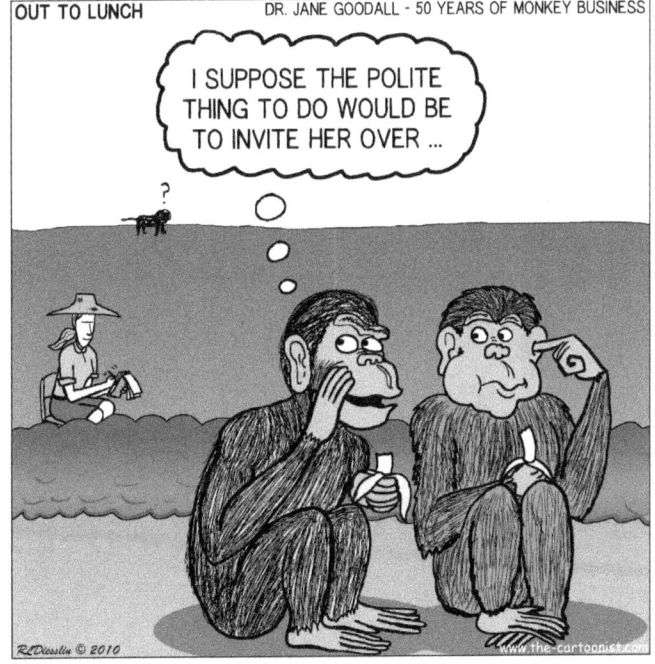

Observations in Nature

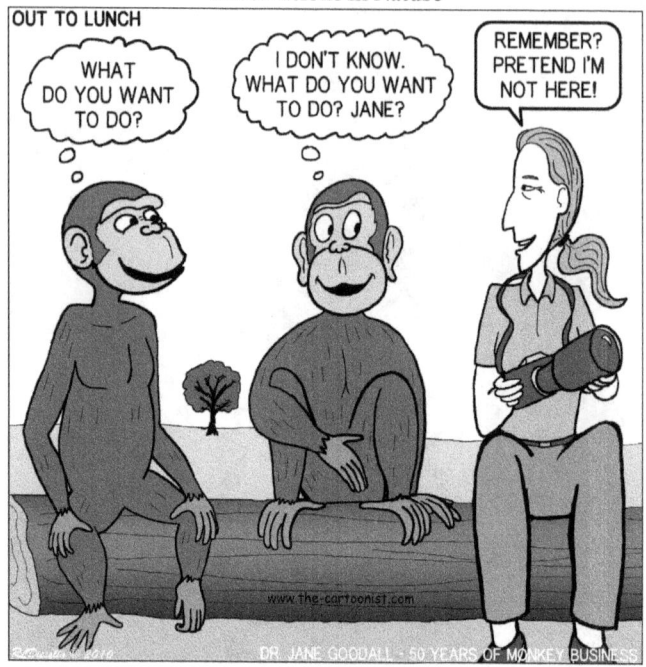

There's No Right Way to Eat a Rhesus

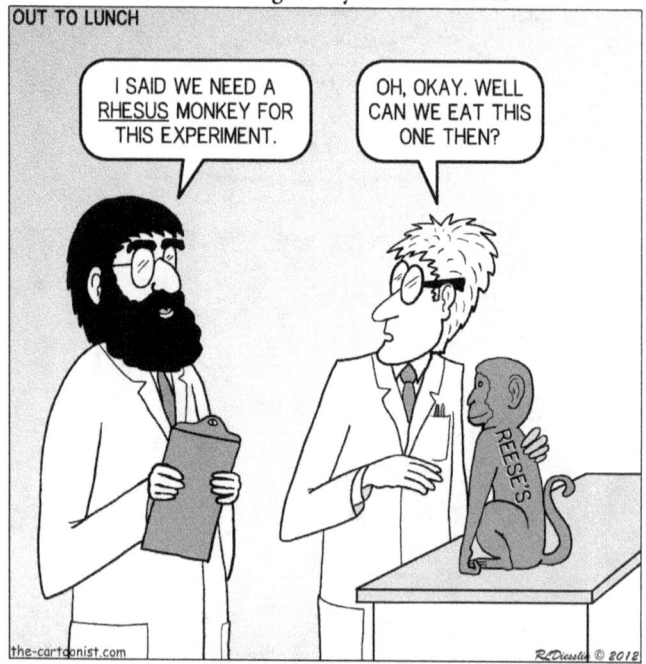

Out to Lunch - Mice and Monkeys - 50

Ostriches, Peacocks and Penguins

Sneaky, Sneaky

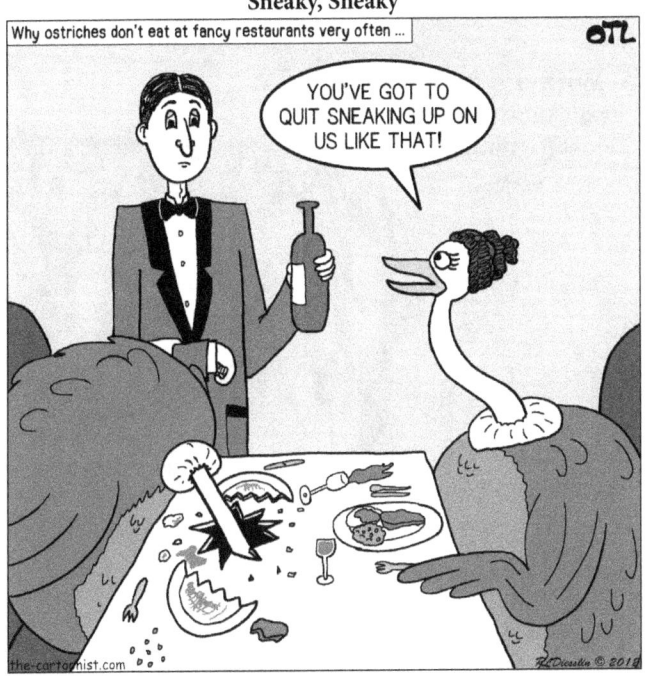

Cold is Cold

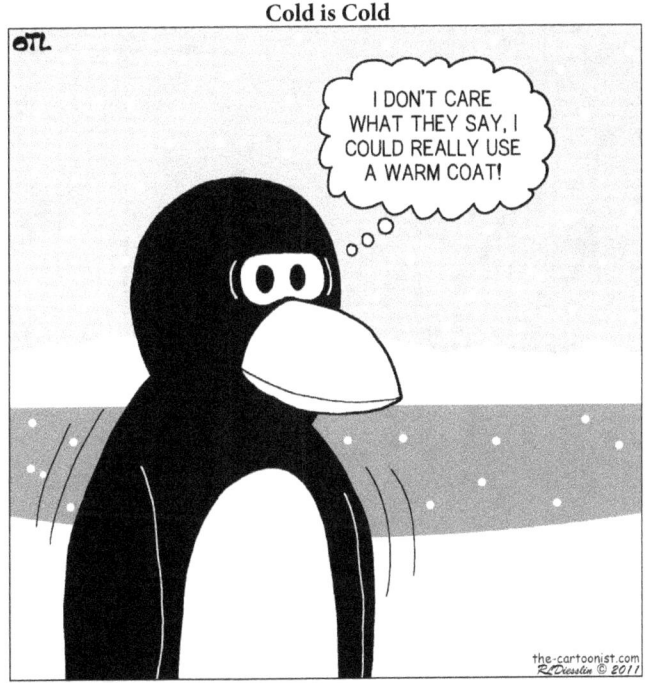

Penguin Mother's Day

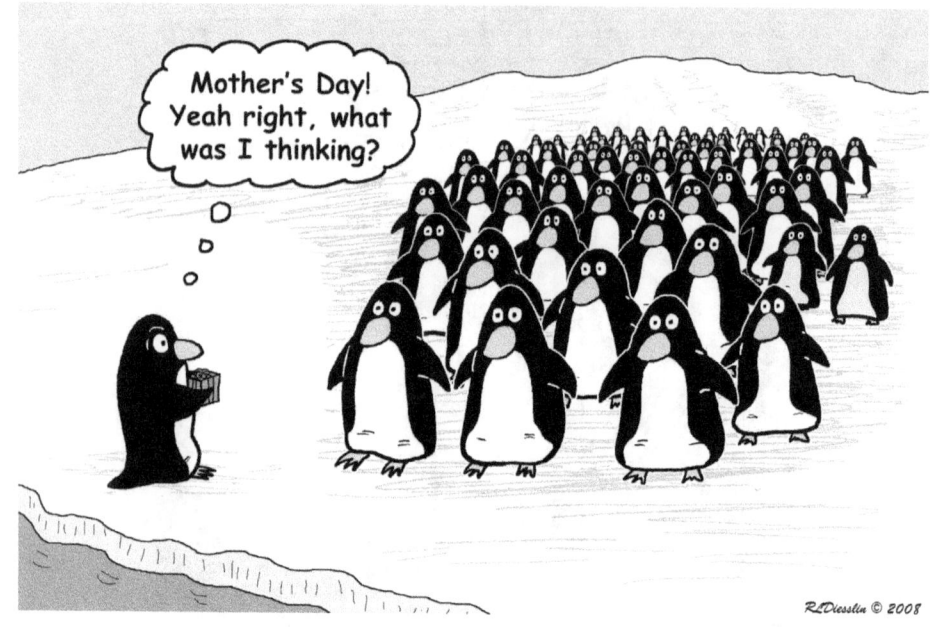

Party Time

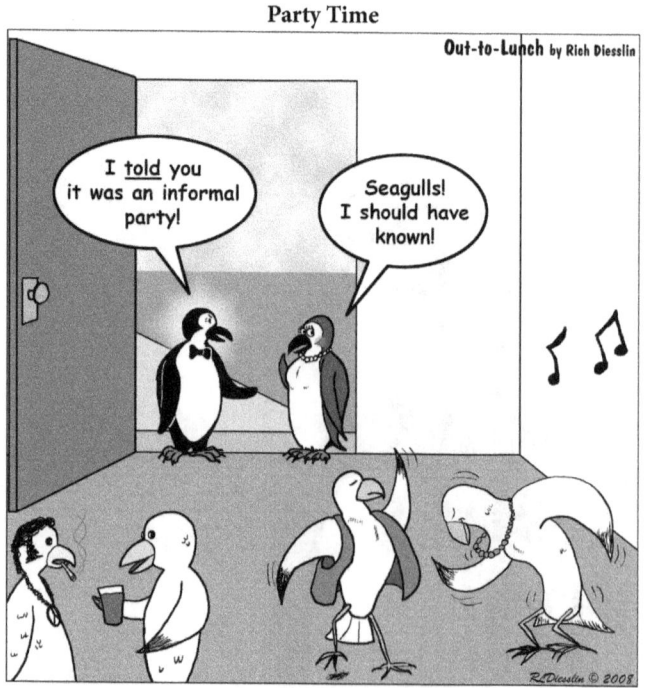

Identity Crisis

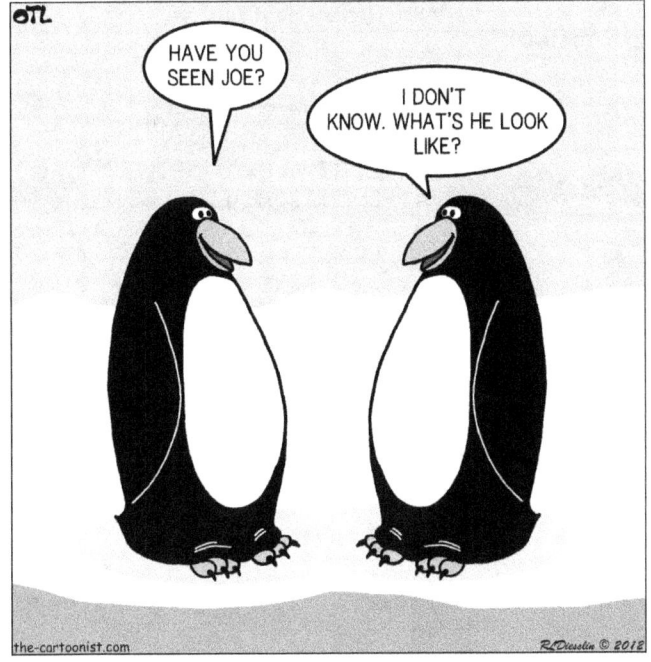

Sea Horses, Sea Otters, Sea Turtles and Sharks

Science Mistakes?

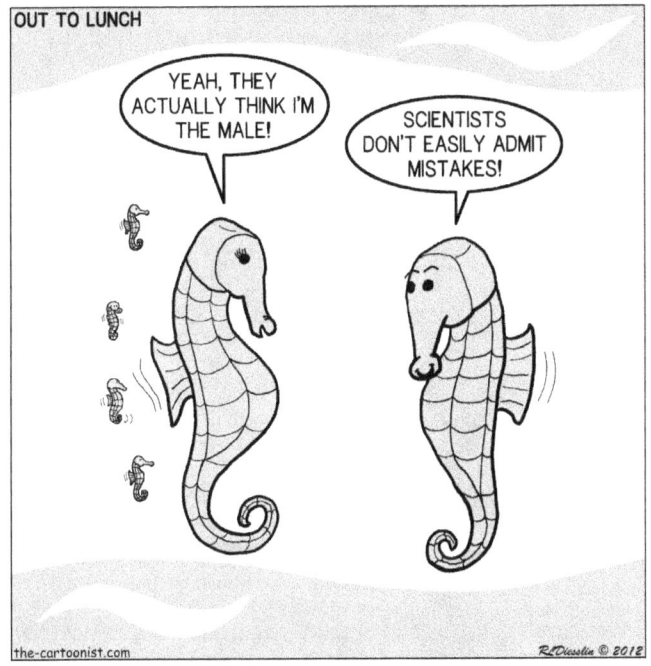

If Sea Otters Could Talk

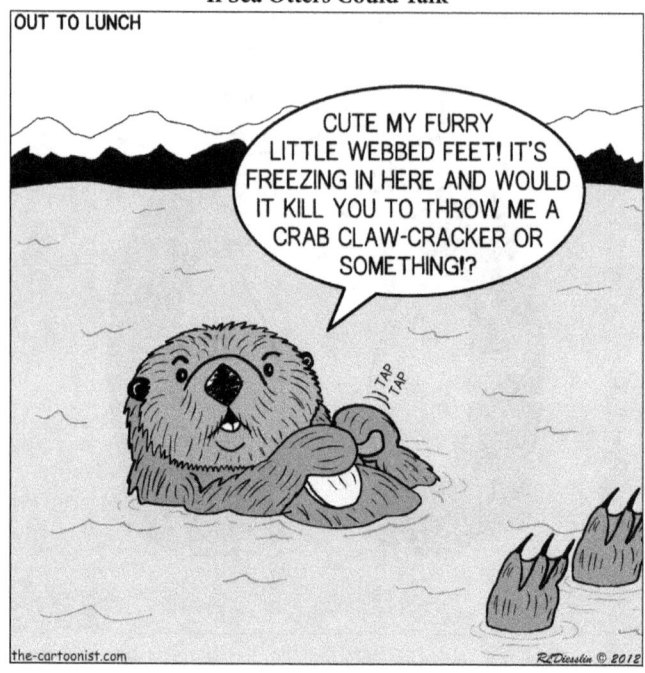

Sea Turtle SCUBA

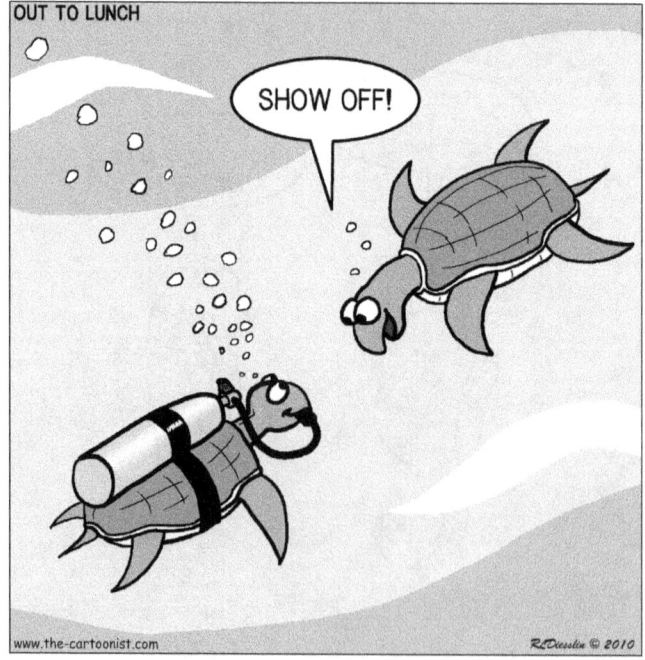

Seafood

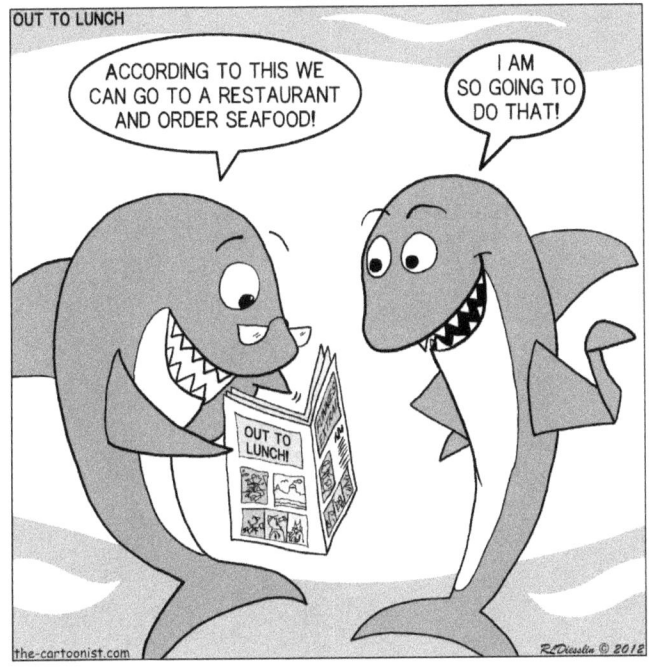

Land Shark?

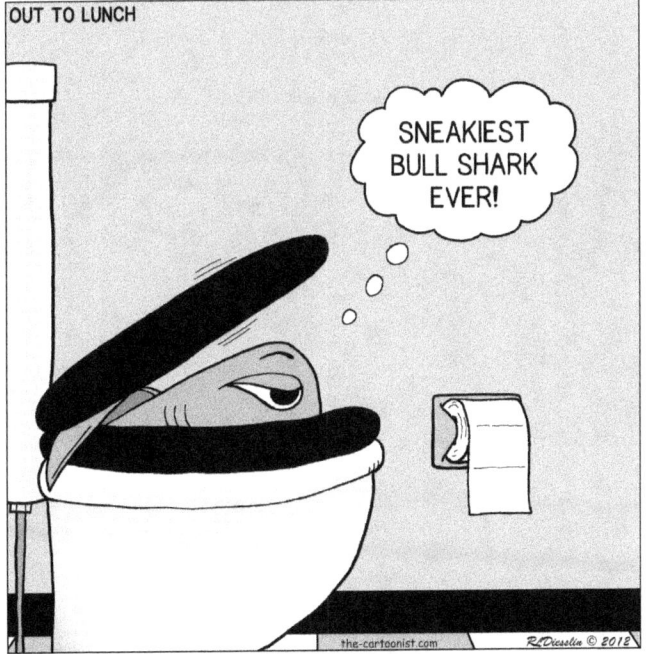

Out to Lunch - Sea Horses, Sea Otters, Sea Turtles and Sharks - 55

Fair Weather Friends

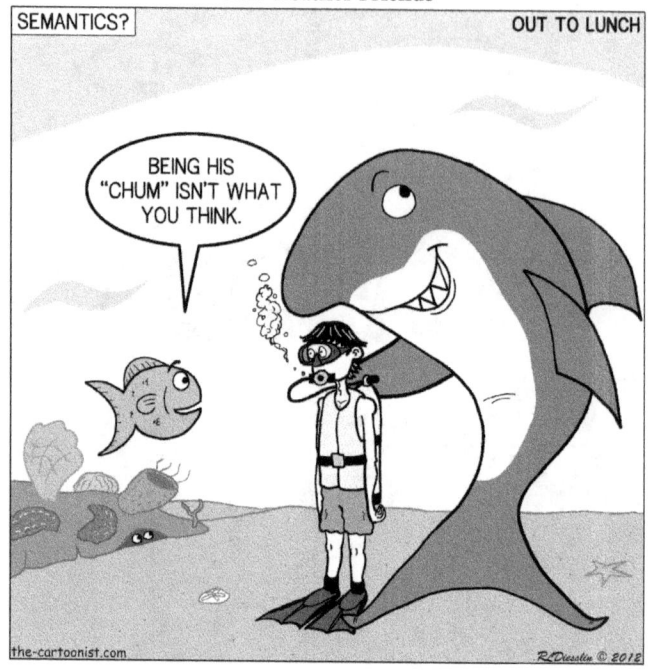

It's Not a Moray (aka Pilot Fish)

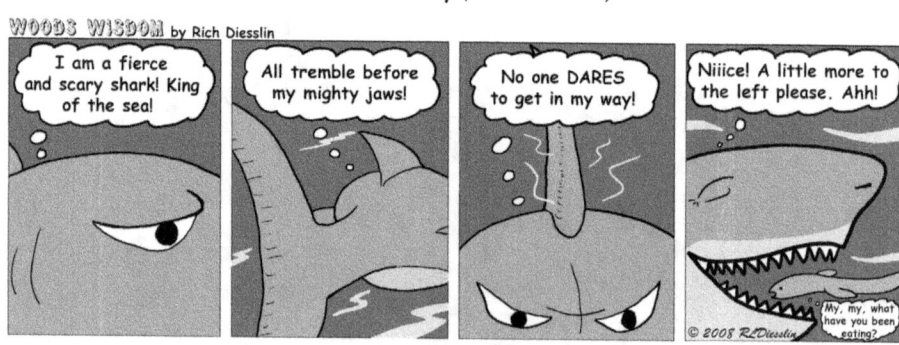

The Eyes Have It

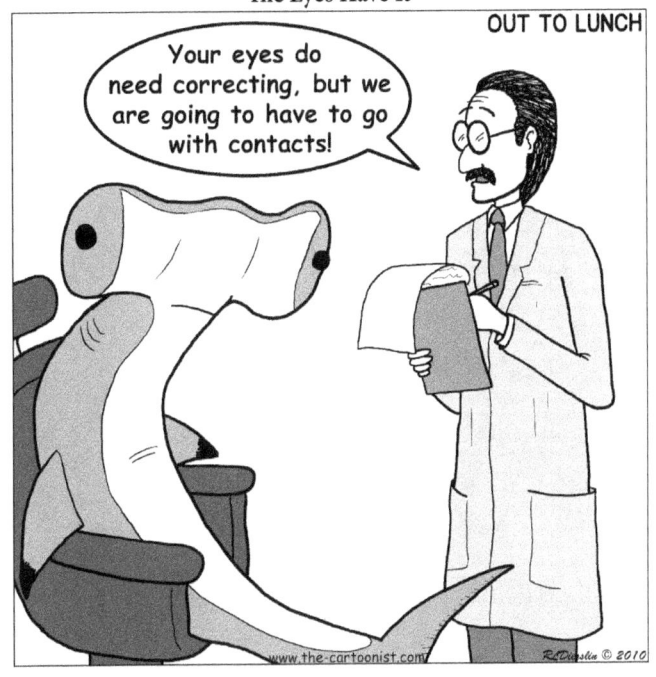

Book Club

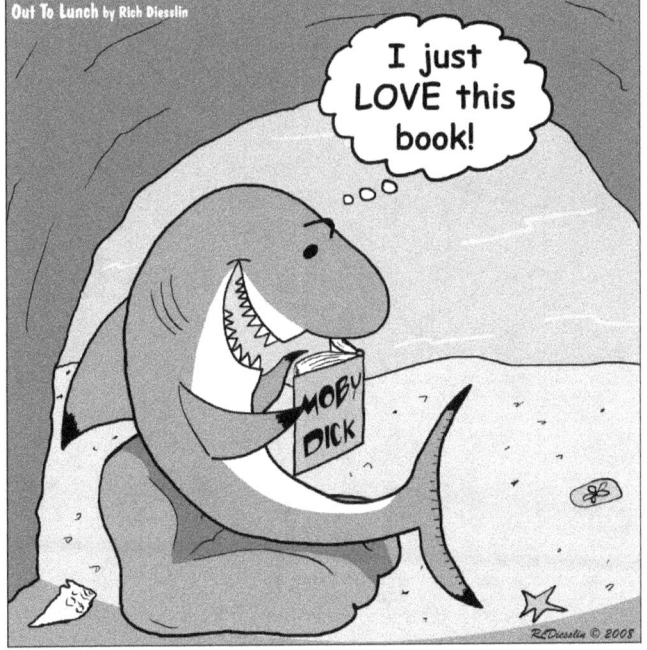

Touchy

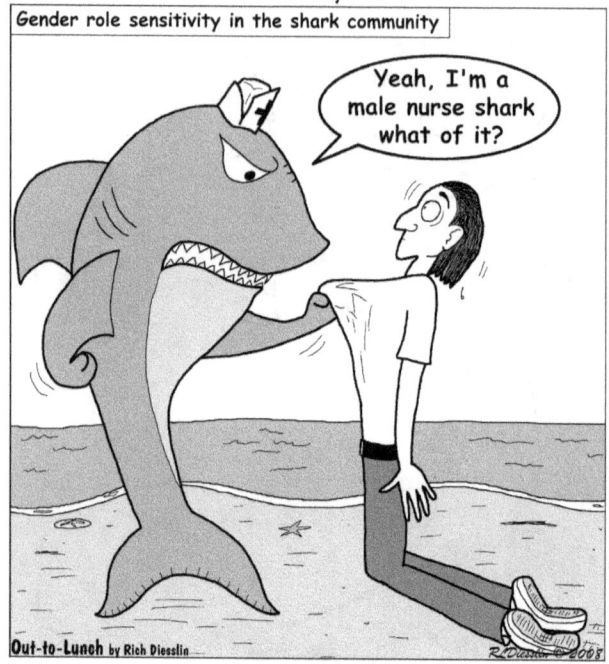

Lifeguard

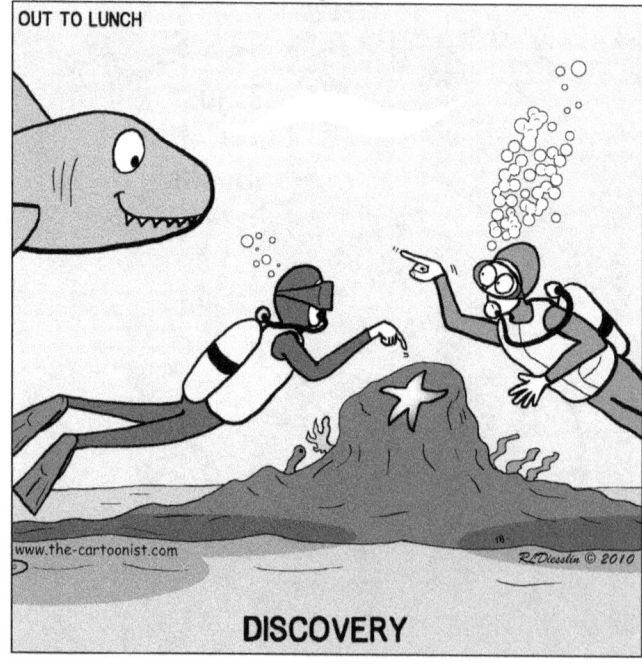

Skunks, Snails and Snakes

Skunk Favorite Sandwiches

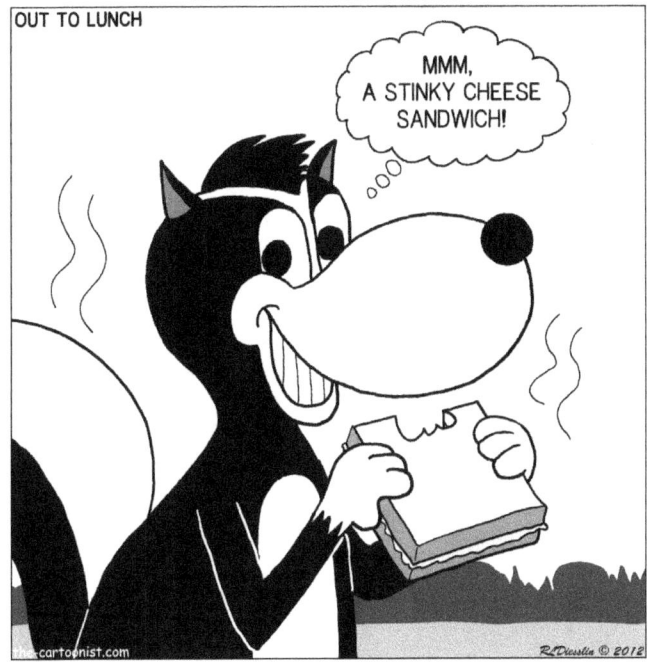

Chemical Warfare

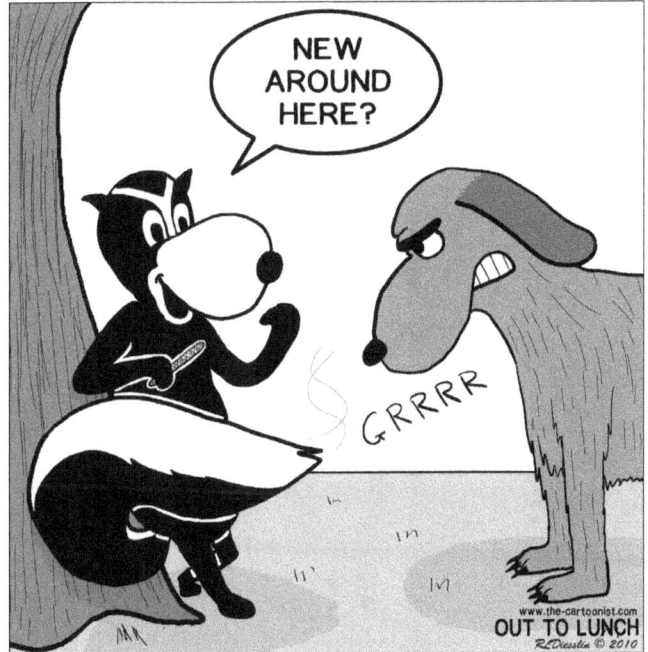

Scientist Faux Pas

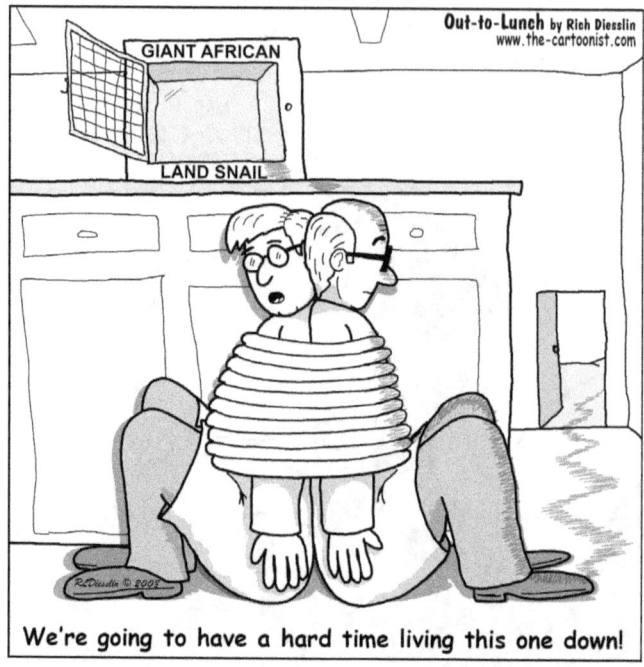

We're going to have a hard time living this one down!

Watch Your Asp

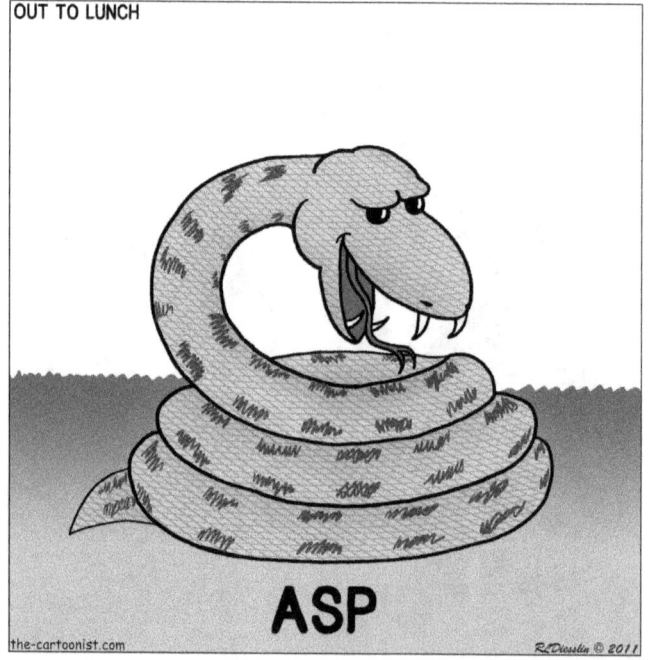

Takes One to Know One

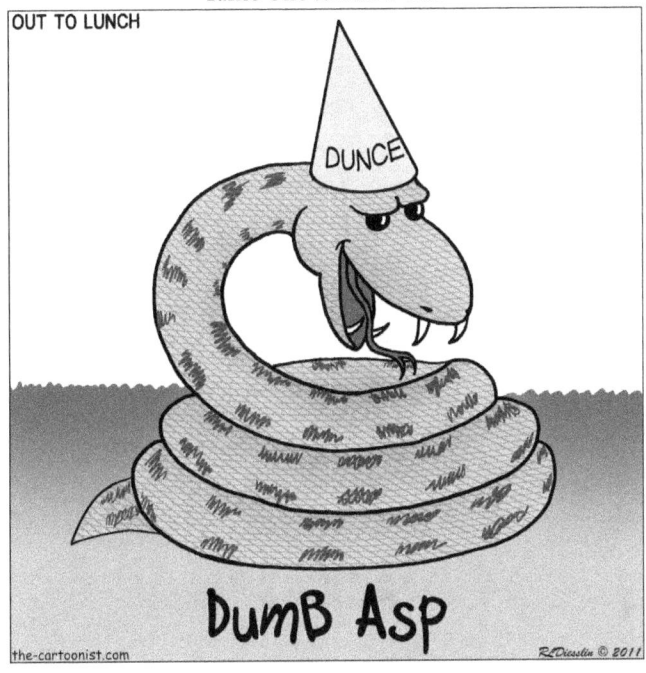

Eating the Elephant One Bite at a Time

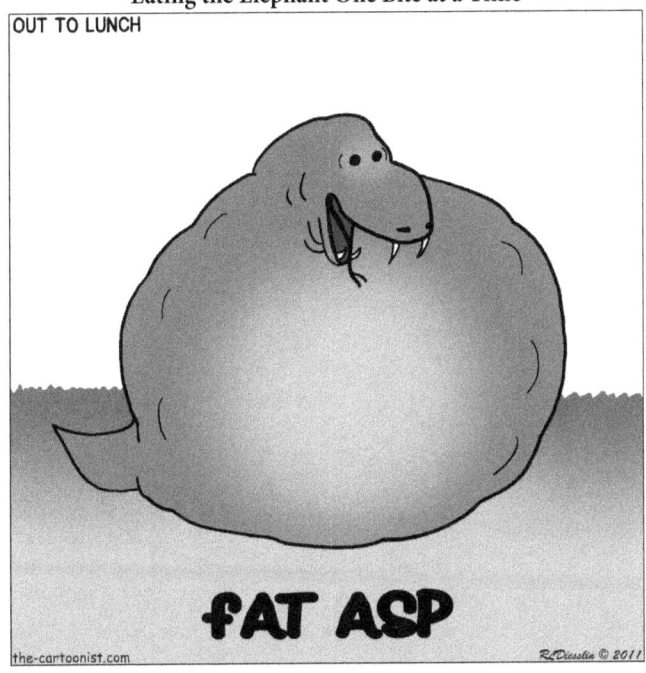

Getting Off Your Asp

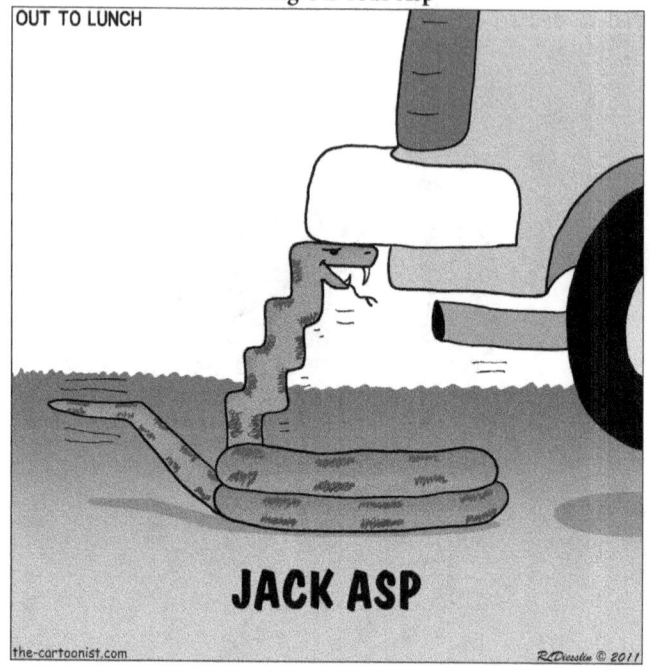

Gradumacated and Everything

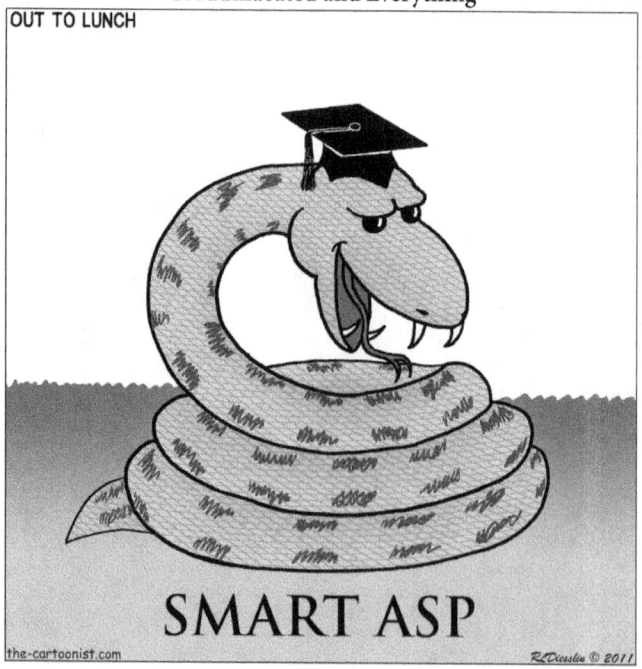

Yet Another Bad Asp Joke

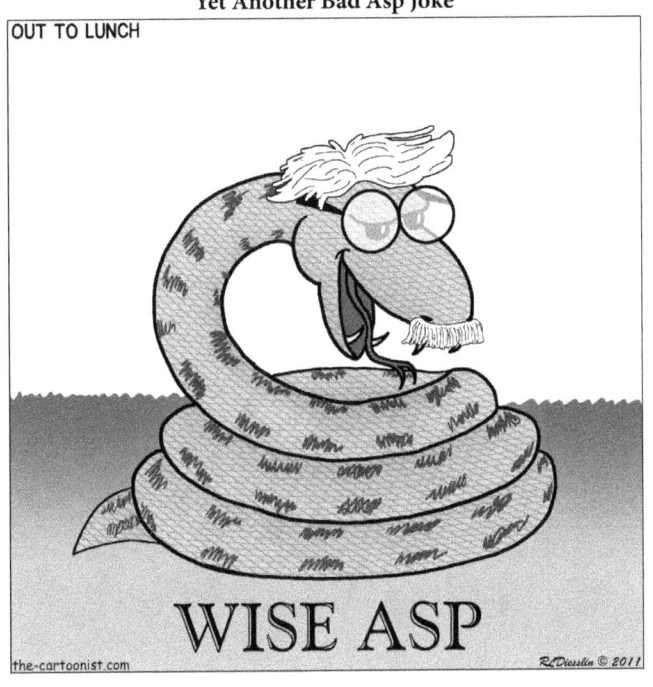

Snake Moods

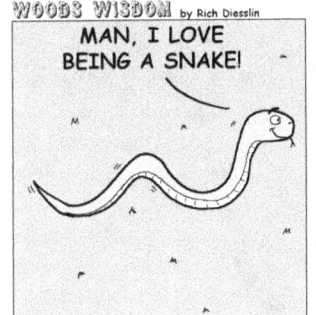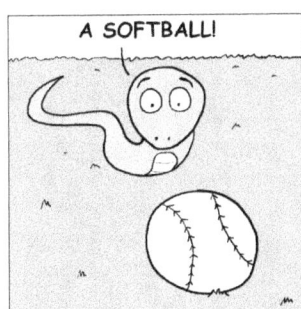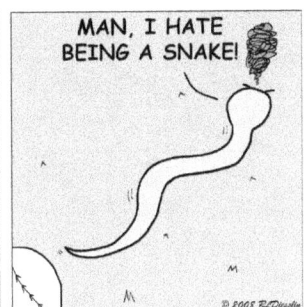

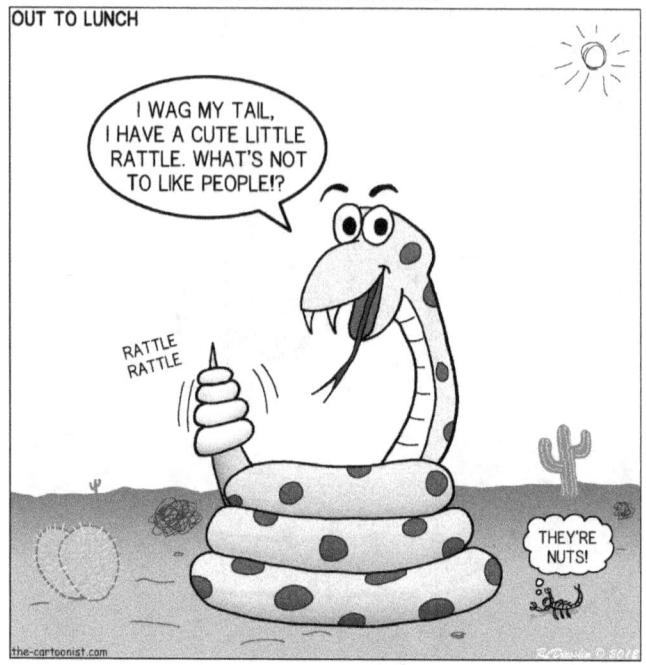

Spiders, Sponges, and Squid

Problems of a Real Spider Man

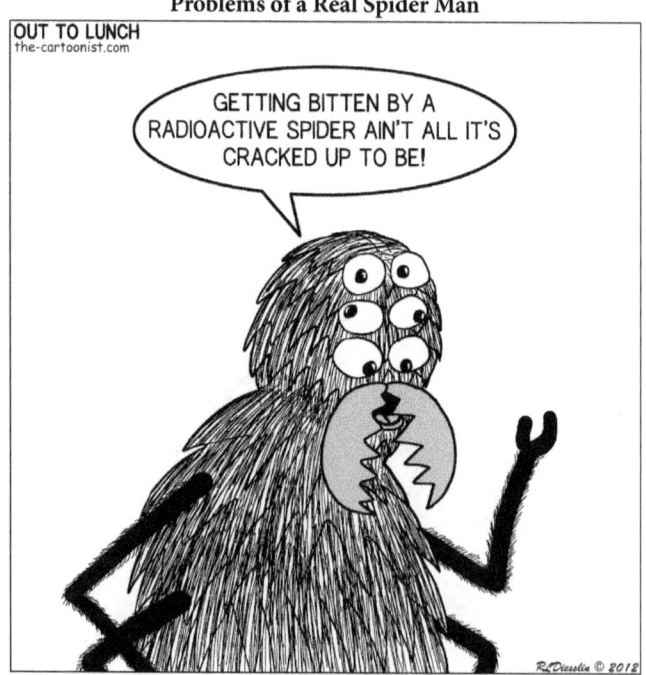

Spider Delusions of Grandeur

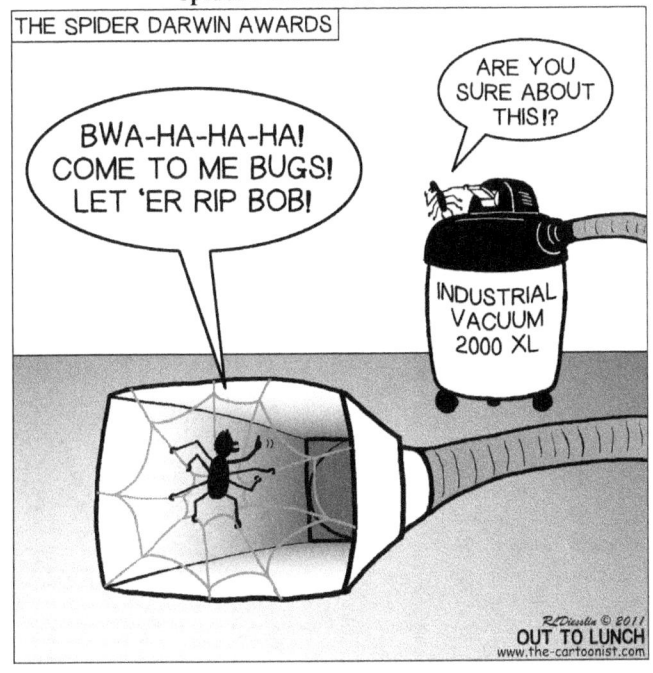

Father's Day Problems

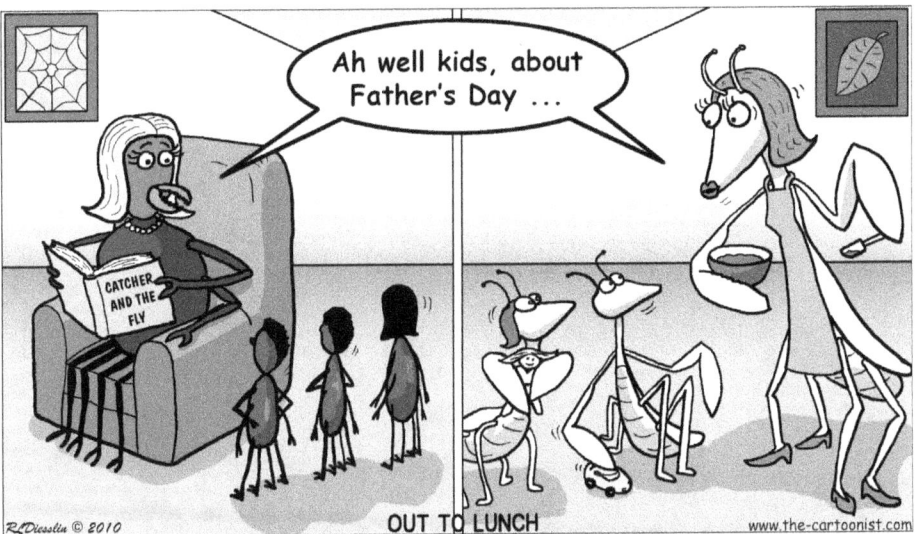

Fisher-Man

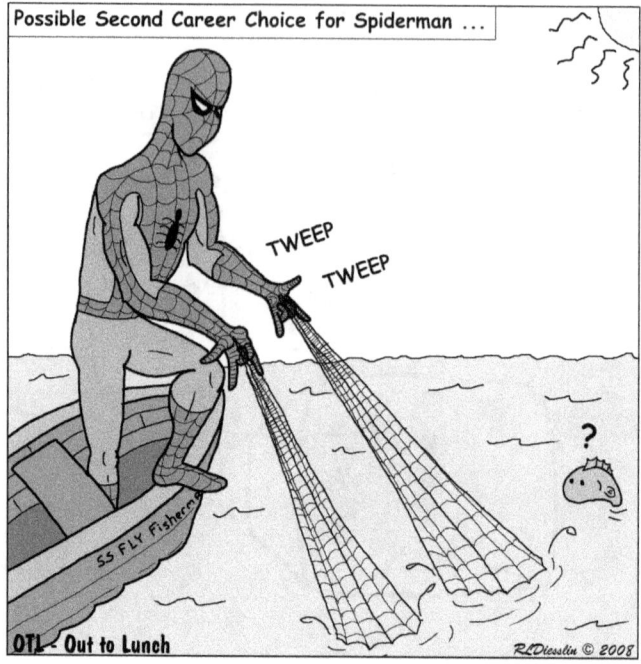

Spiderman Favorite Snacks

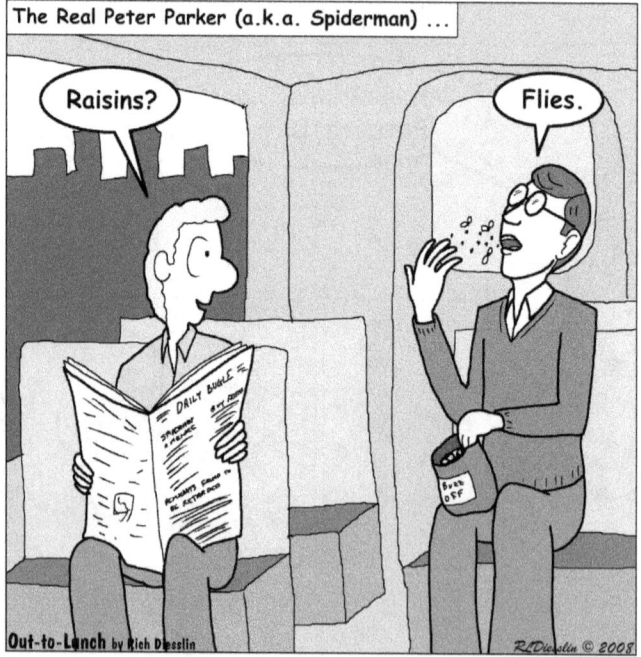

Soak it In

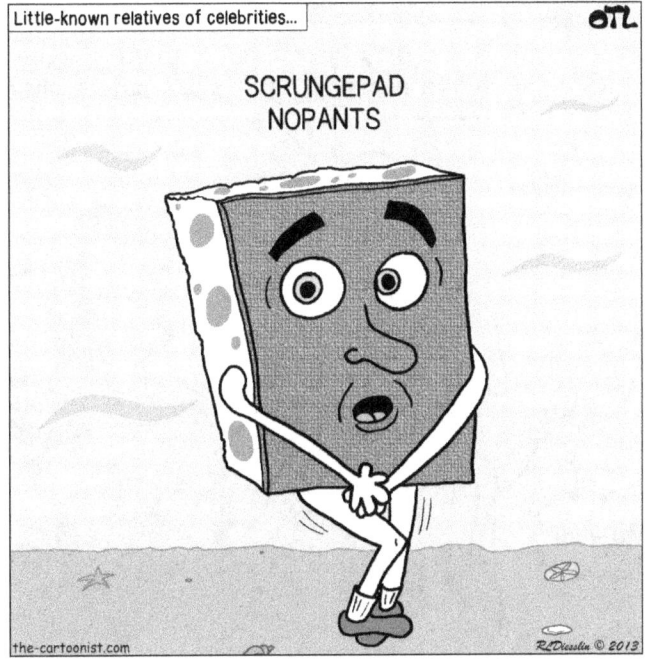

Squid Baseball Players

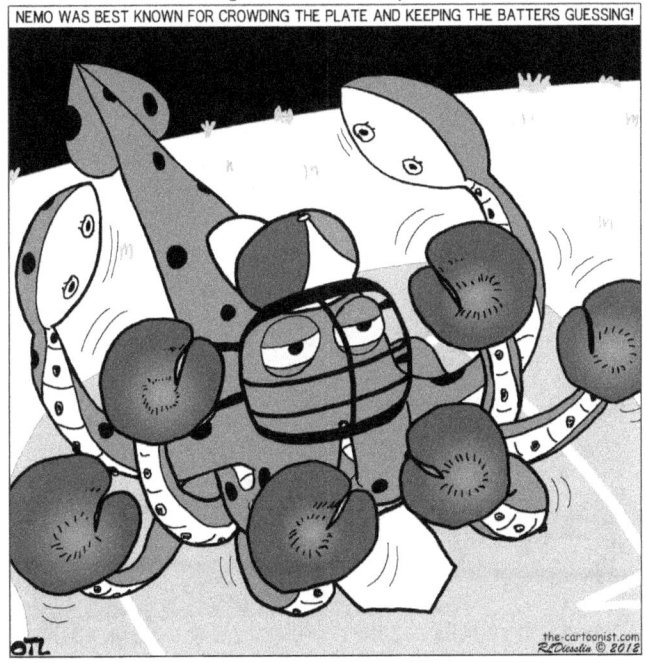

Rough Delivery

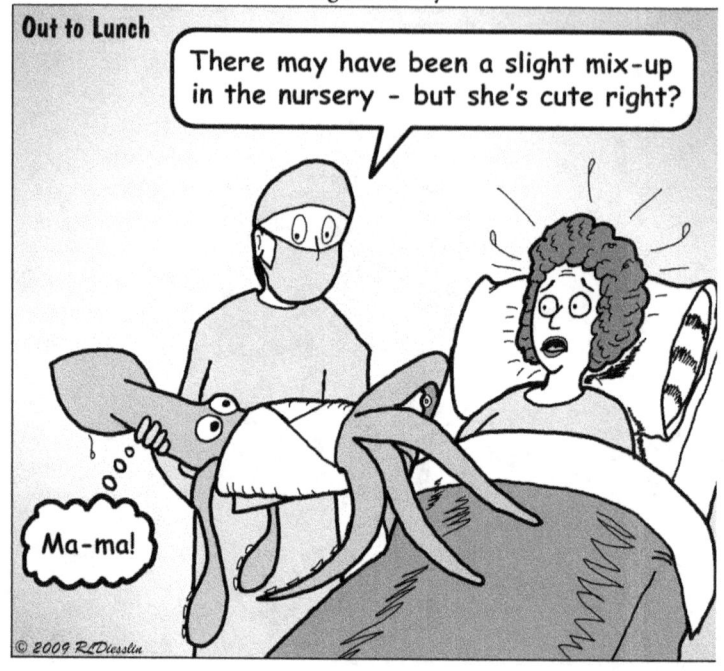

Ring Around the Collar

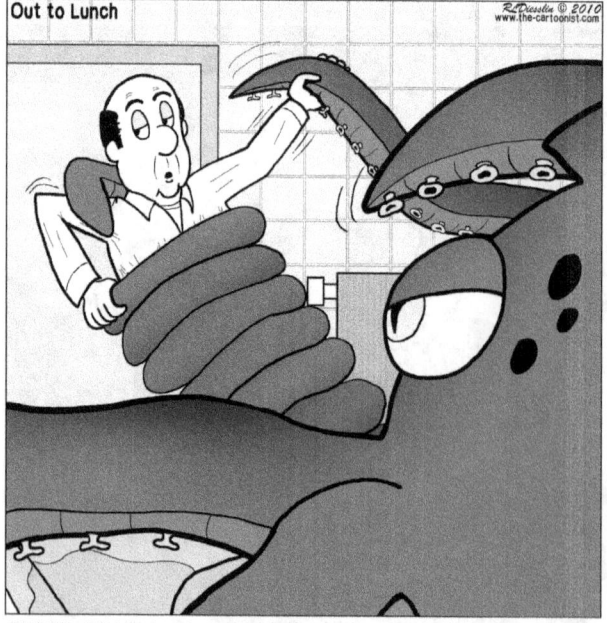

A Sticky Situation

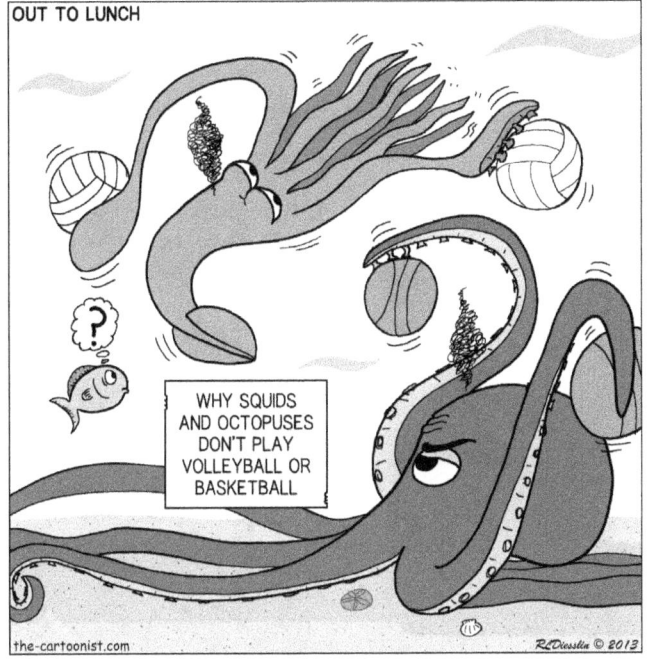

Squirrels, T-Rex and Turkeys

Base Jumping

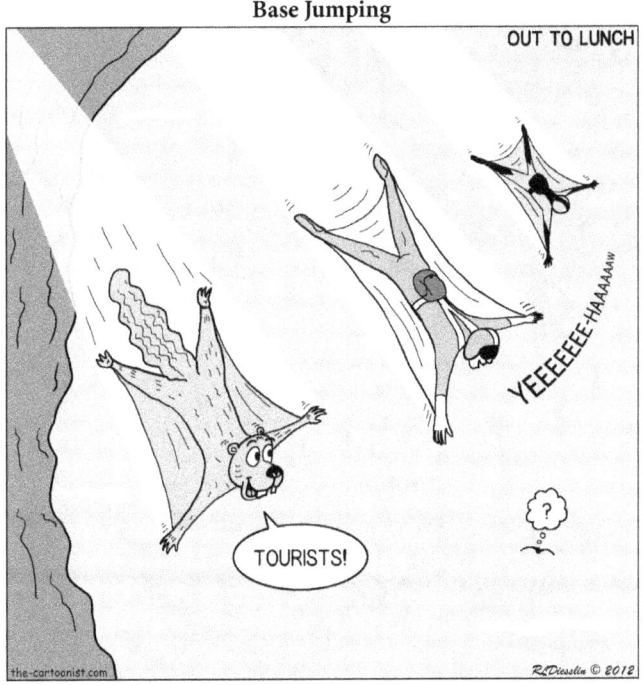

Animal Timeshares

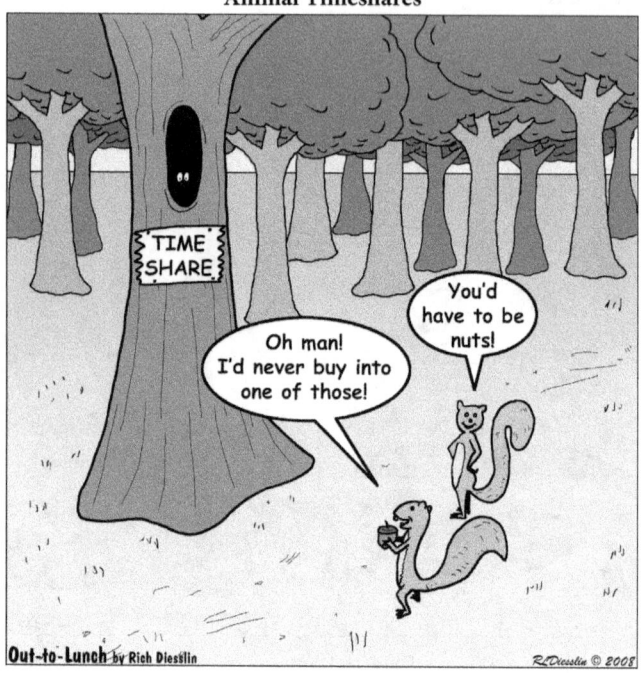

T-Rexting

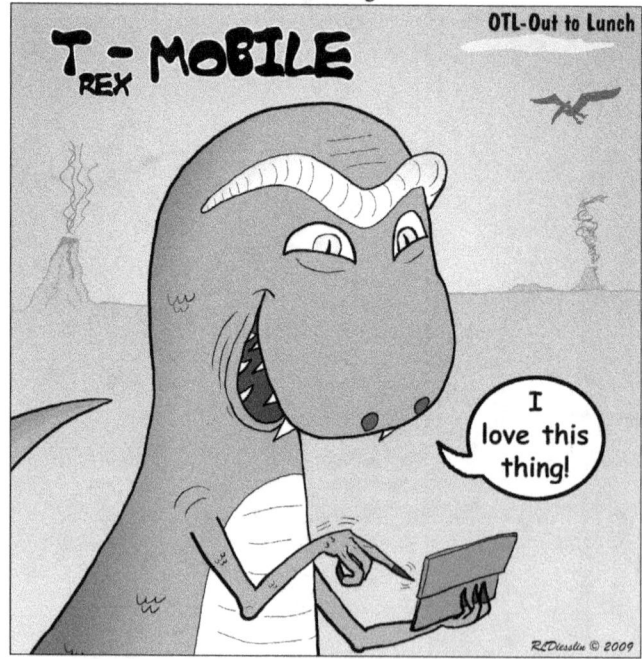

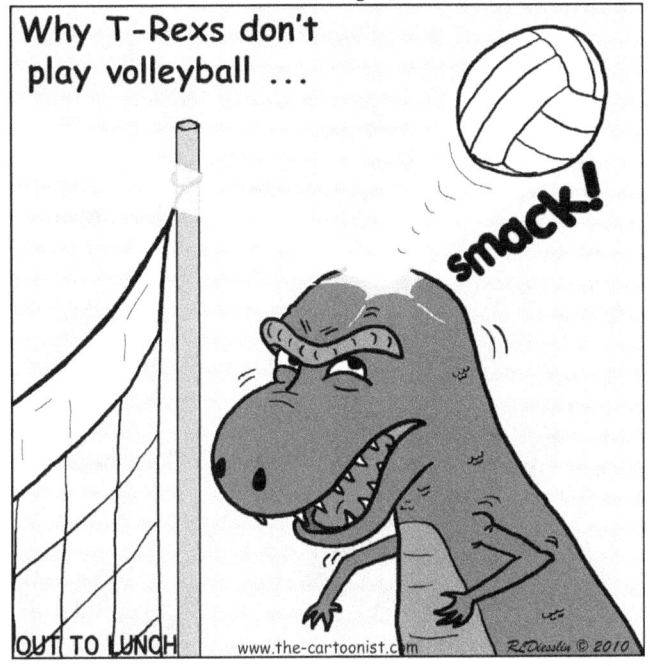

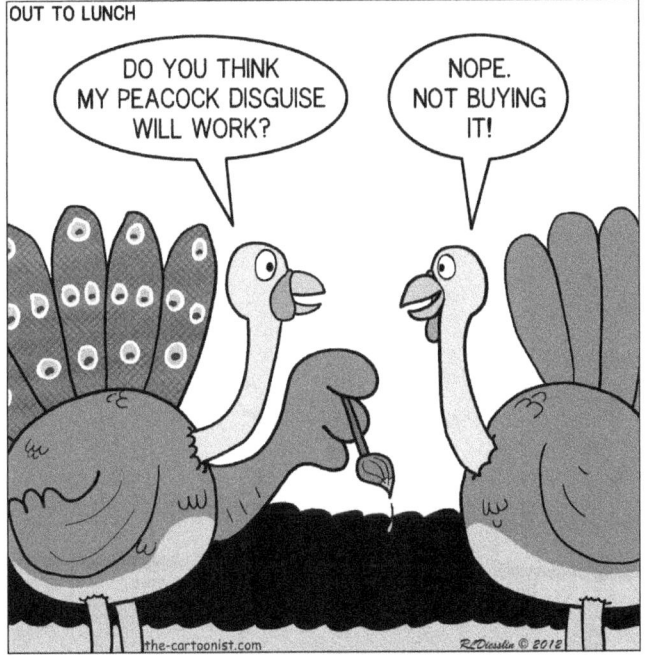

Whales

Ahab Visits the Wailing Wall

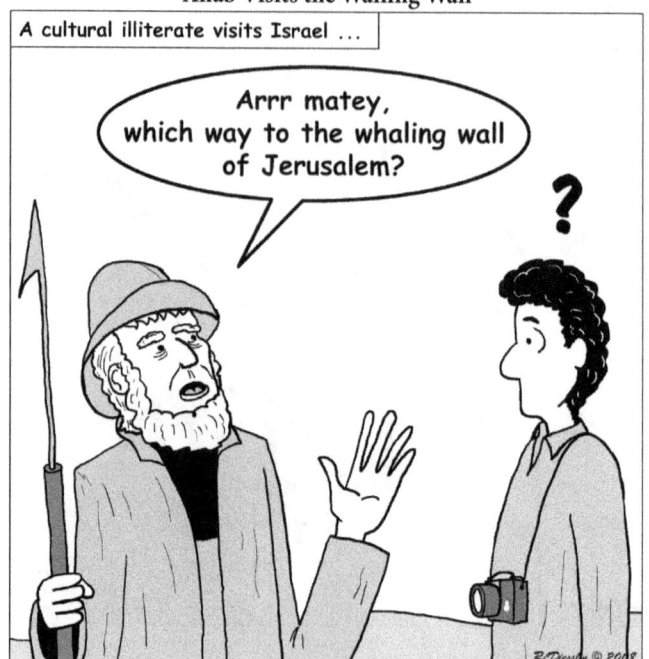

Moby Dick Follow-up Visit

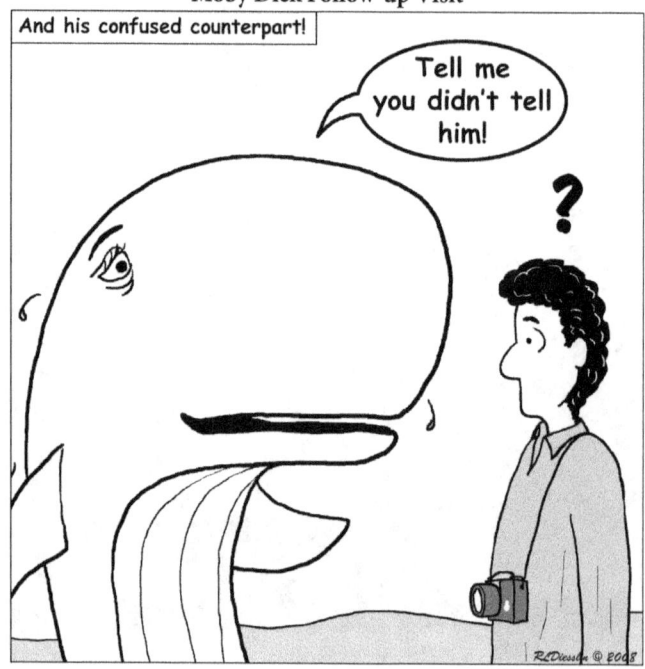

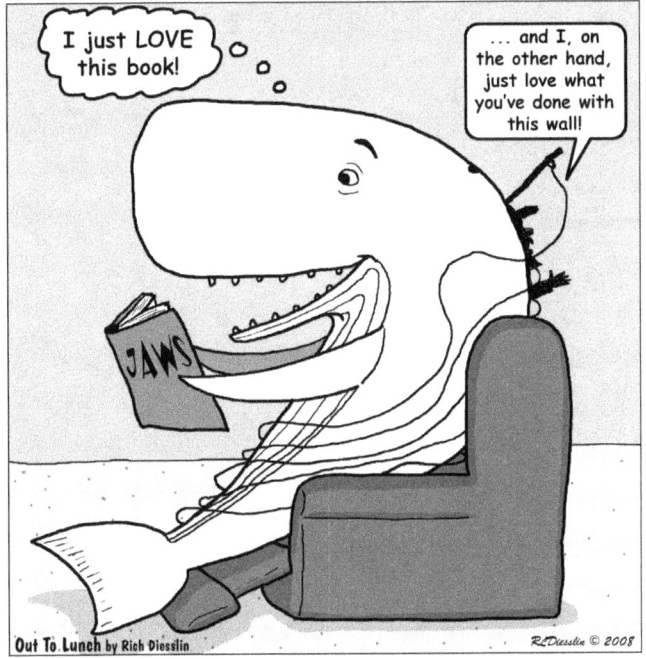

Christmas Animals

Eating Us out of House and Home

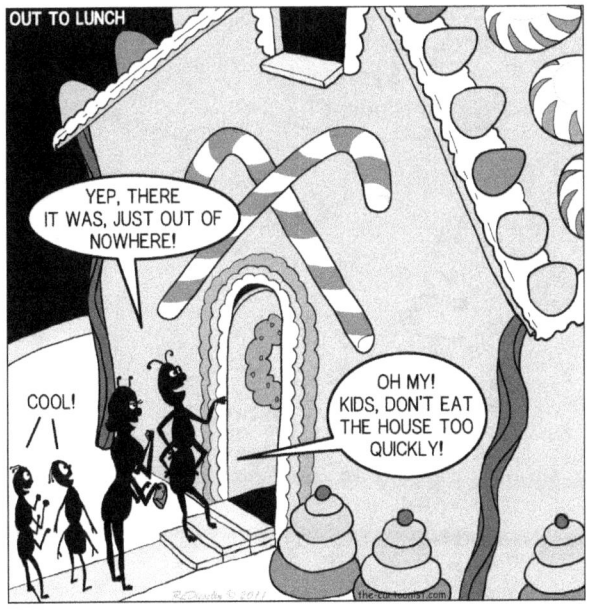

The Cat in the Hat Comes Back

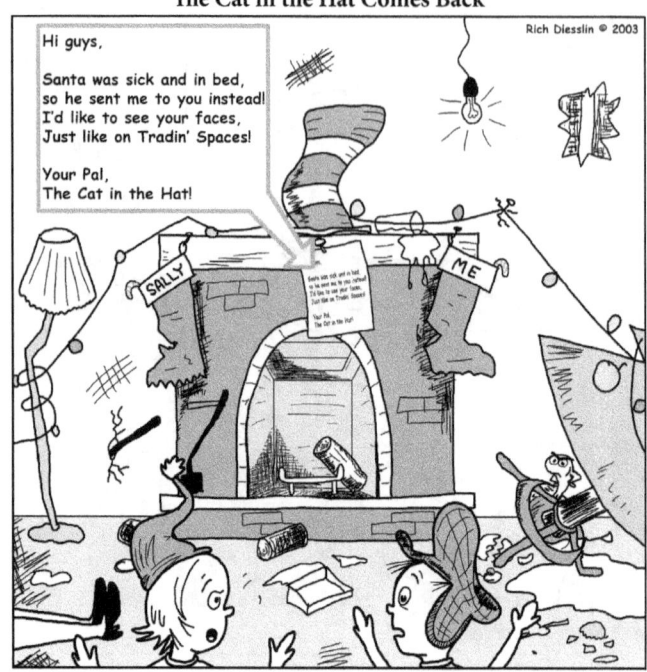

Inappropriate Reindeer Gifts

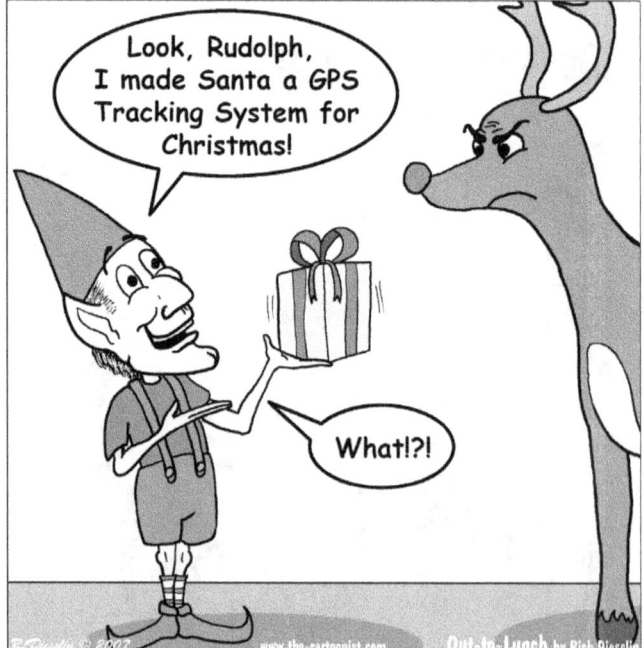

Rudolph's Dilemma

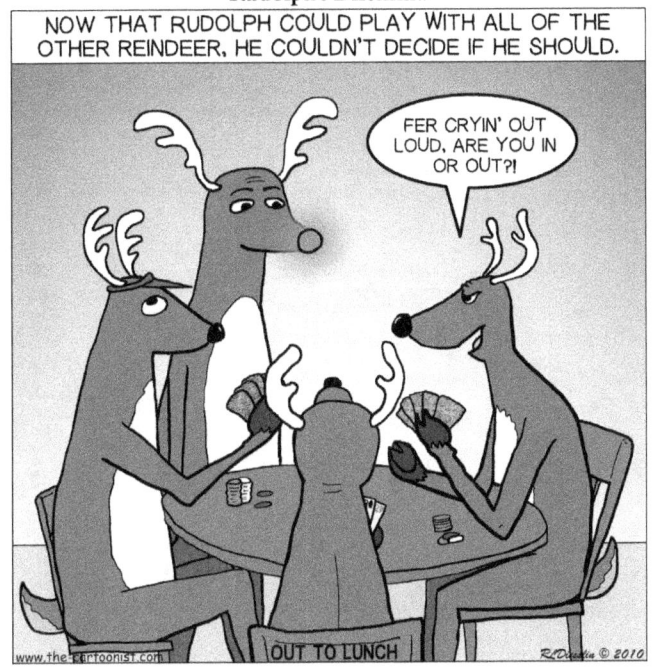

Reindeer Hunter

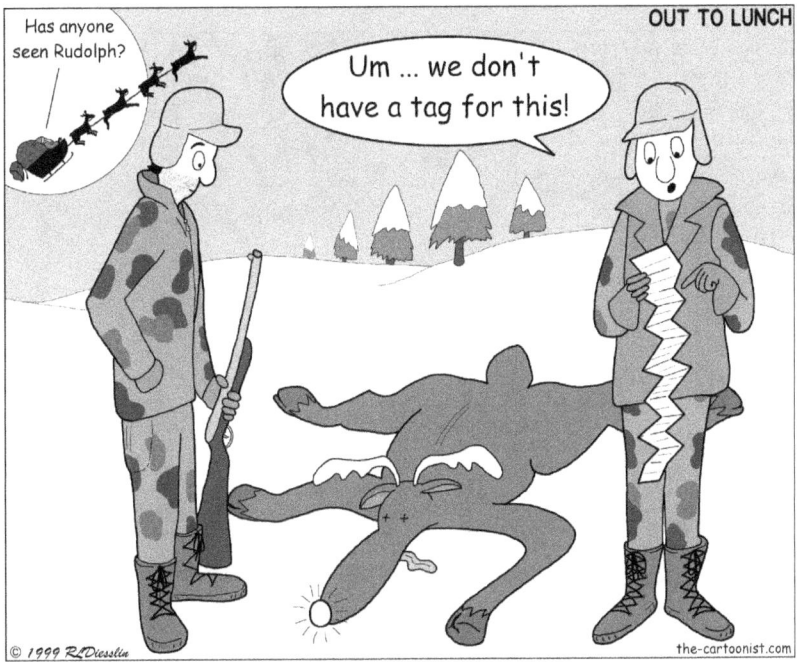

Someone's Been Bad

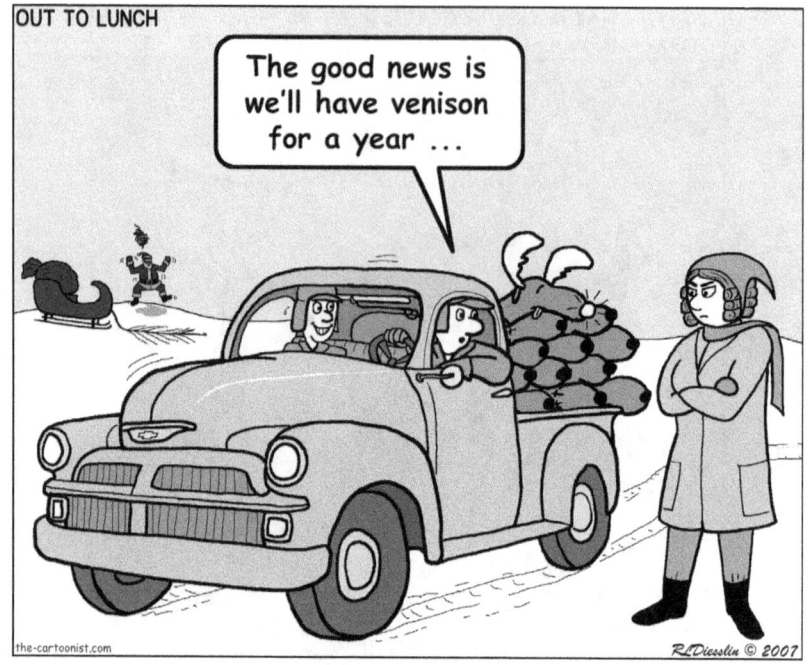

Mouse Musings

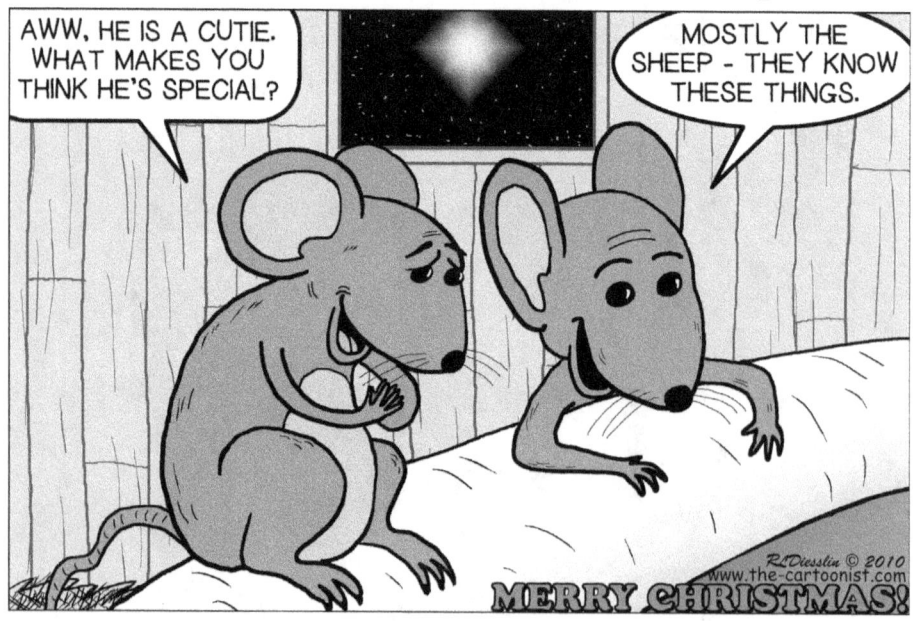

Improbably Pairings

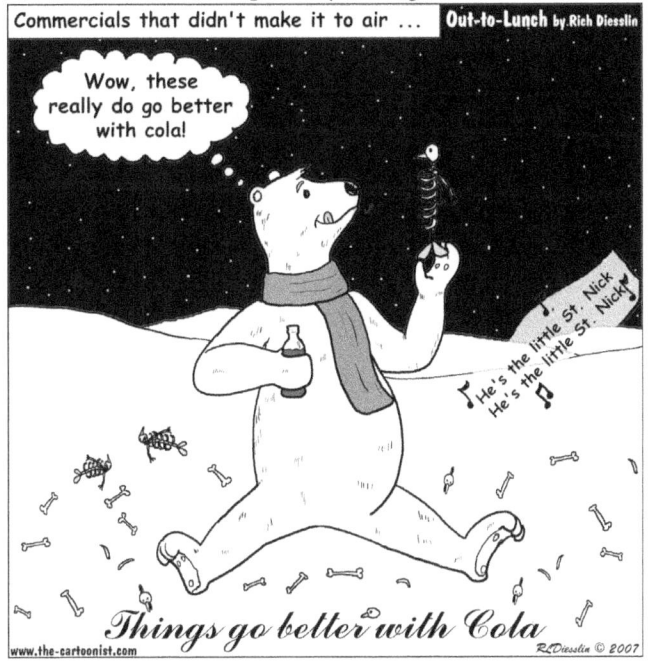

Keebler Elves?

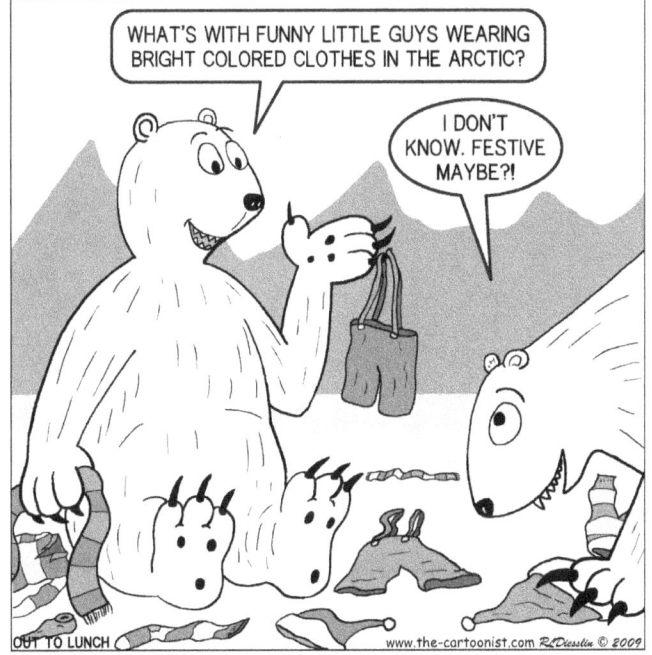

Bi-Polar

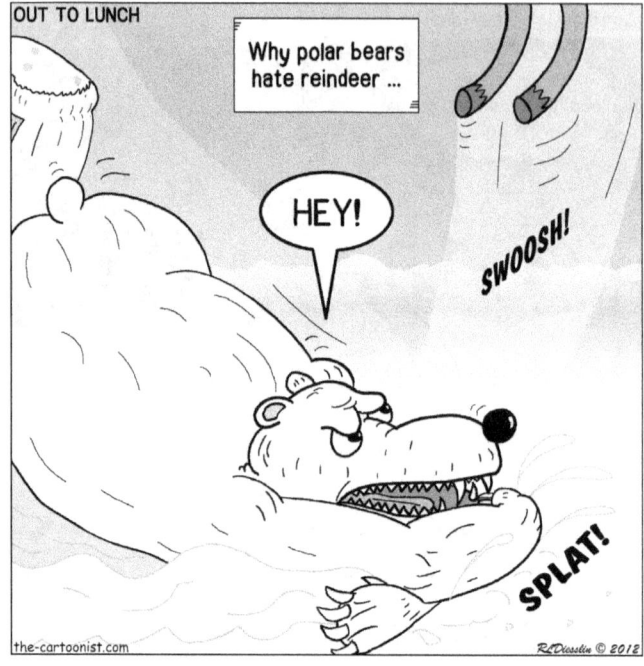

Home Video Bad Ideas

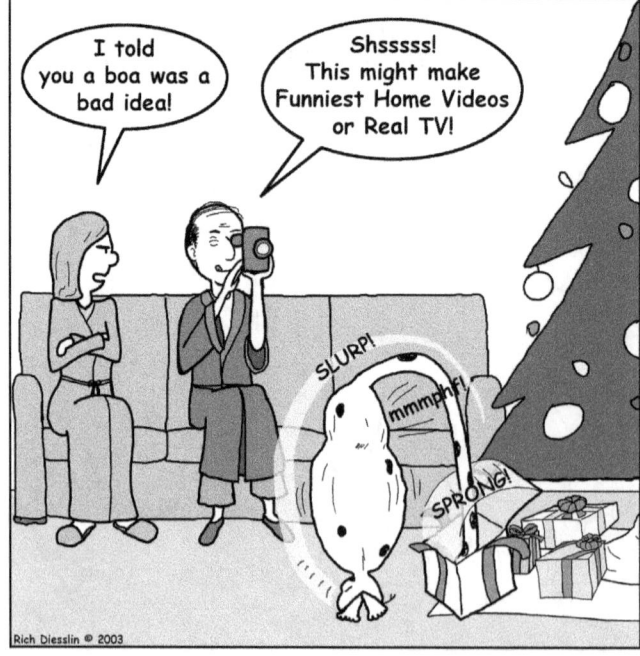

Squid-o-Clause

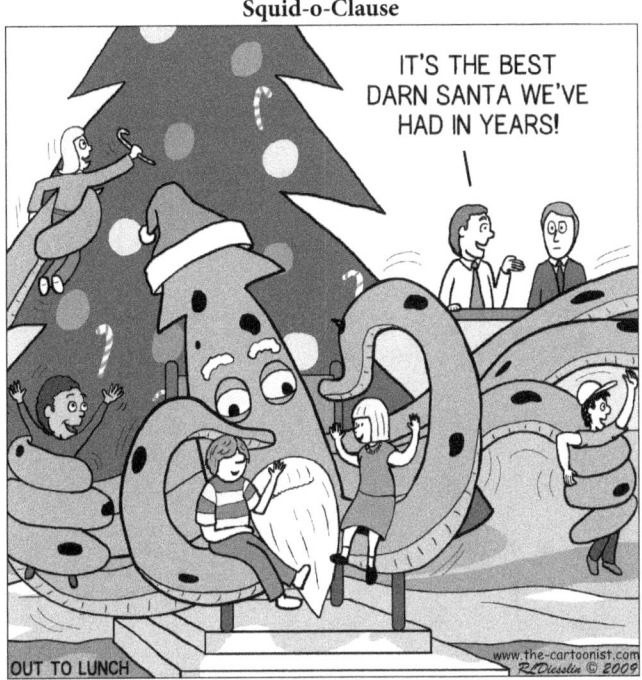

Bonus: Selected Animal Cartoons of the Old Testament

Well, that's all the OTL animal cartoons for now but, as a bonus, here's a look at some animal antics from The Cartoon Old Testament.

The Cartoon Old Testament (COT) is a commentary exploring Old Testament scripture passages from the common lectionary via cartoons and musings (shameless plug for that book). Anyway, enjoy this sampling of some of the animal-related cartoons ...

Fording the River

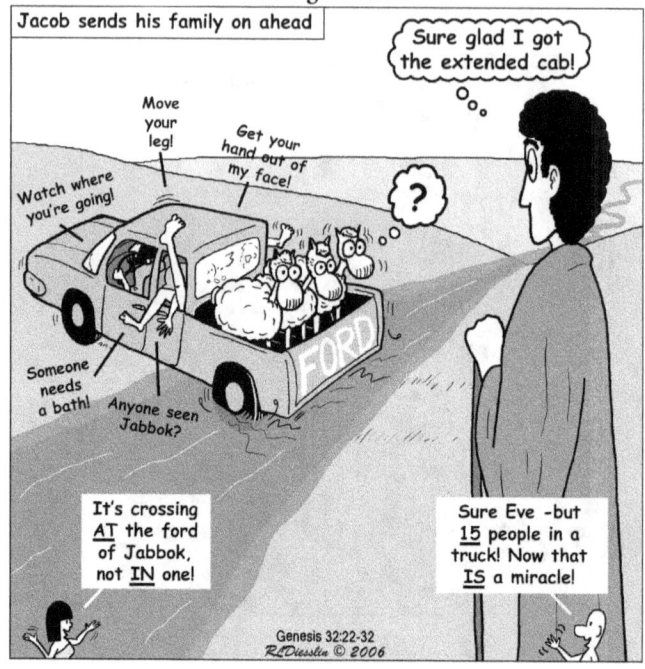

The Lion and the Lamb

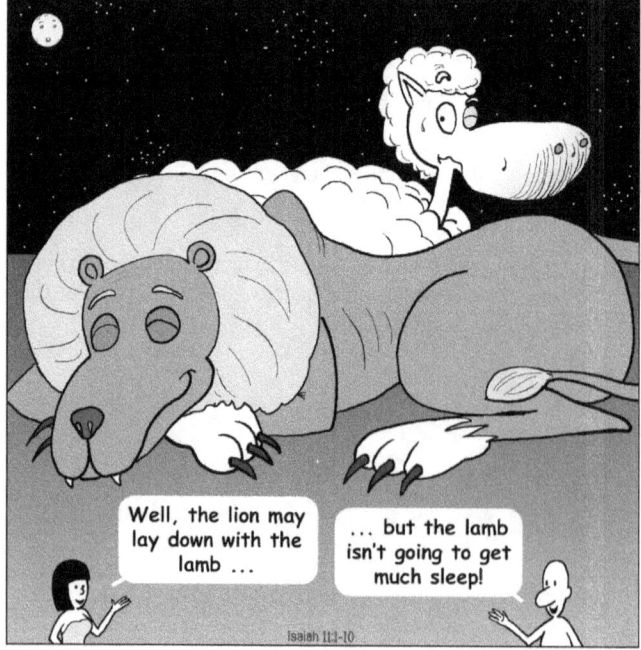

Early Outdoor Worship Services

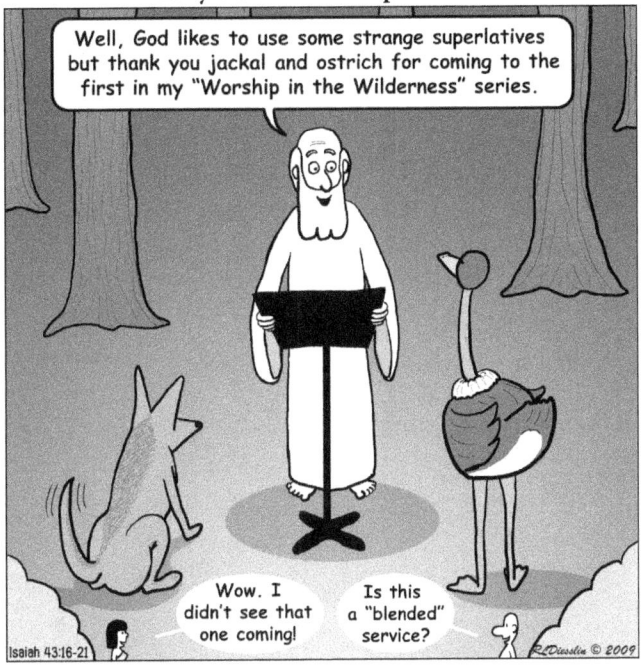

Unusual Military Strategies

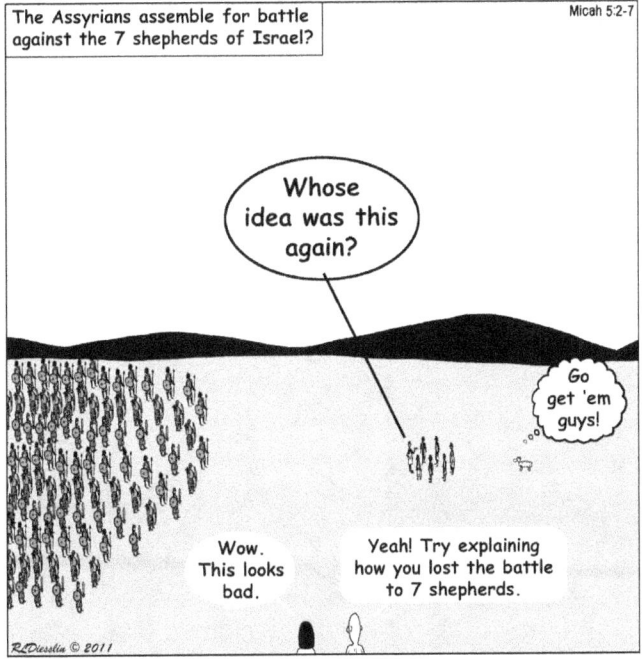

Bonus: Selected Animal Cartoons of the New Testament

Also as a bonus, here are some animal-related cartoons from The Cartoon Gospels.

In similar fashion to the Cartoon Old Testament, the Cartoon Gospels are cartooning of gospel scripture readings (and another shamelss plug for a great book).

Selected here are a few of the animal related cartoons. Enjoy!

God's Diet Plan

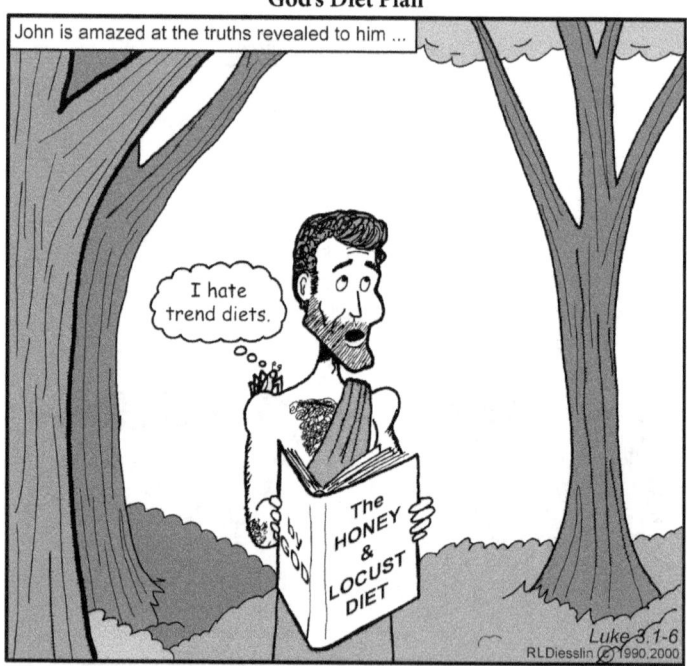

You're kidding ... right!?!

Recruiting Disciples

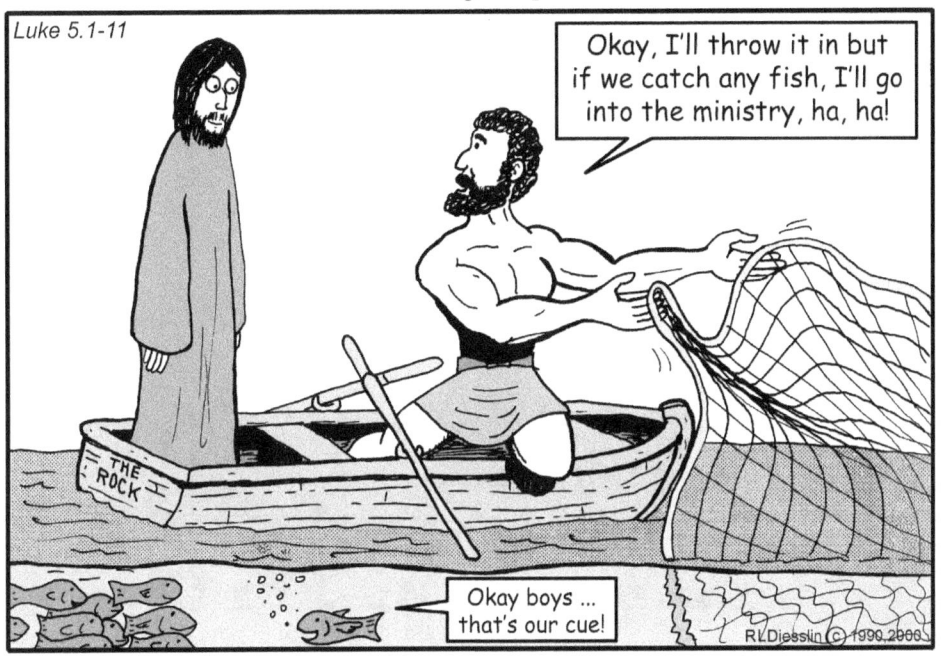

Snake Bad PR

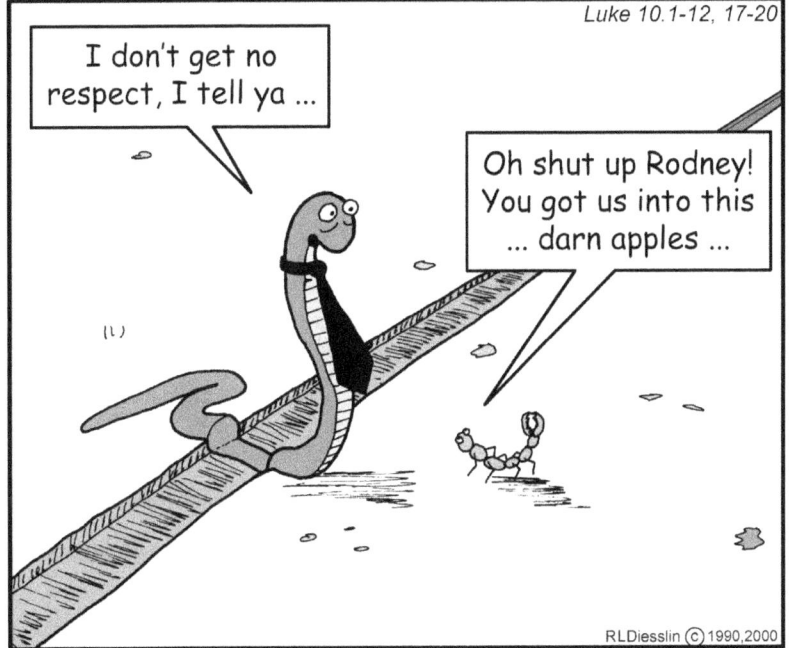

Foxy

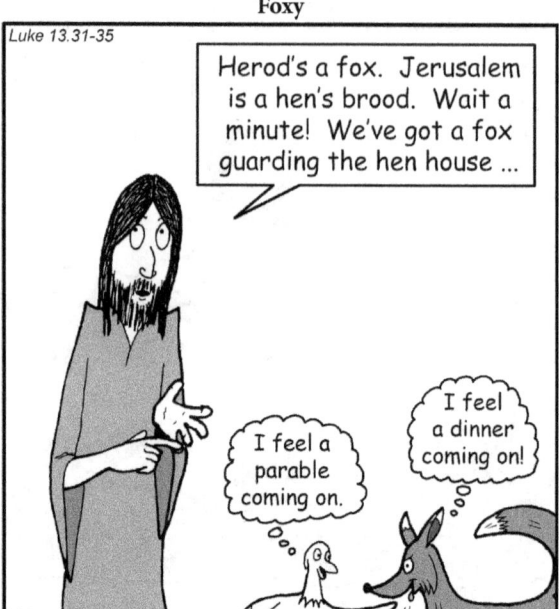

The stuff parables are made of.

A Case of Mistaken Identity

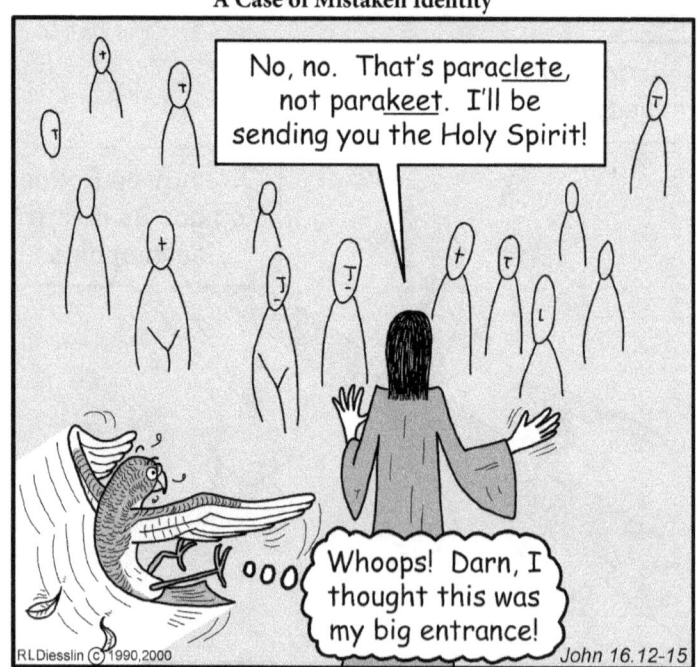

The End!

I hope you liked this collection of Out to Lunch animal cartoons a bonus material. Thanks for your interest in my cartoons!

You can follow OTL online at www.the-cartoonist.com or maybe someday in your local paper. Most of these cartoons are also available on cheesy merchandise such as t-shirts, sweatshirts, coffee mugs, cards, posters, clock, trivets, key chains, quilt squares, pen holders, mouse pads and more through my Cafe Press Shops and on Amazon.Com! So if you haven't wasted enough money on the book already, that might be a good way to go. Always here to help!

All the Best,
Rich

Other Books by the Cartoonist

Books in Print

The New Classics, 21st Century Comic Strips, ISBN: 978-1481143738, Los Vegas:Ink Bottle, November 2012, b/w paperback, 148p, 500+ cartoons!

Out to Lunch, Cartoons with an Appetite for the Ridiculous, ISBN: 978-0-9848872-1-7, Dayton:Diesslin Press, February 2012, 170+ cartoons, black-and-white paperback.

The Cartoon Old Testament, Cartoons and Commentary on the Old Testament, ISBN: 978-0-9848872-0-0, Dayton:Diesslin Press, June 2011, 164p, black-and-white paperback.

KNOTS Cartoons, Celebrating the Fun in Scouting, ISBN: 978-0-9702244-8-4 Dayton:Diesslin Press, April 2010, 80p, full color paperback.

A Journey Through Christian Theology, Minneapolis:Fortress Press, ISBN: 978-0-8006969-7-9, March 2010, 2nd Edition. Editor/Author William P. Anderson.

The Cartoon Gospel of John, A Serious Commentary with Visual Parables, ISBN 0-87946-273-6, Chicago:ACTA, September, 2004, 128p. Commentary written by William P. Anderson.

The Cartoon Gospel (of Luke), ISBN 0-940169-09-6, New Berlin:Liturgical Publications, Inc., December, 1990.

E-Books and Cartoon Collections

The New Classics, 21st Century Comic Strips, December 2012, 500+ cartoons, b/w Kindle ebook.

Out to Lunch, Cartoons with an Appetite for the Ridiculous, February 2012, 170+ cartoons! Full color kindle ebook or pdf.

The Cartoon Old Testament, Cartoons and Commentary on the Old Testament, ISBN: 978-0-9702244-9-1, Dayton:Diesslin Press, June 2011, 164p, full color Kindle ebook or pdf.

KNOTS or Not Scouting Cartoon Collection, (cartoons on CD for newsletters, etc.), ISBN: 978-0-9702244-6-0, and annual supplements, cartoons from 1999 through 2012.

KNOTS Cartoons, Celebrating the Fun in Scouting, April 2010, full color Kindle book or pdf.

Joseph: A Tale of Two Traditions, ISBN 0-9702244-7-8, February, 2007.

The Cartoon Ten Commandments, ISBN 0-9702244-2-7, October, 2000.

The Cartoon Gospels, ISBN 0-9702244-5-1, September, 2002.

The Cartoon Gospel of Mark, ISBN 0-9702244-4-3, September, 2002.

The Cartoon Gospel of Matthew, ISBN 0-9702244-3-5, October, 2001.

The Cartoon Gospel (of Luke), ISBN 978-0-9702244-1-5, December, 1990.